"In *Shepherd Leadership*, the authors develop at once a highly imaginative and yet compellingly practical analysis and stories of successful leadership practices. Its remarkable insights are valuable for current and aspiring leaders at all levels of the organization. A great tool that, because of its focus on spiritual principles, adds to the considerable body of literature on leadership."

☛ *J. McDonald Williams, chairman emeritus,
Trammell Crow Company*

"Experts on leadership have made up all sorts of models for it—from coach to orchestra conductor and beyond. McCormick and Davenport have found a relevant and useful model from a time-honored image, that of a shepherd. Their book will challenge your thinking and, more importantly, make you a more effective leader."

☛ *K. Terry Koonce, president,
ExxonMobile Production Company*

"Psalm 23 celebrates a lasting and successful leader-follower relationship. Both leaders who take their legacy seriously and followers who want to grow in their leadership knowledge will benefit from McCormick and Davenport's rich exploration of shepherd leadership."

☛ *Ellen Whitener, senior associate dean,
McIntire School of Commerce, University of Virginia*

"McCormick and Davenport's message is that every sheep matters, even you. Every single sheep brings some talent, some unique personality, some contribution to the whole. This work will help you be a better leader and deservedly feel better about yourself and your flock."

☛ *Dr. Michael F. Adams, president, The University of Georgia;
past president, The American Council on Education*

"Today's popular leadership models run the gamut from being a Servant Leader to Attila the Hun. McCormick and Davenport have creatively looked backward in history to help us move forward in our own thinking about leadership. Drawing on ancient wisdom they propose the ground-breaking model of the Shepherd Leader. This quick and engaging read offers fresh insights into both leadership thinking and a classic Psalm."

☛ *David W. Miller, president, The Avodah Institute*

Shepherd Leadership

Blaine McCormick
David Davenport

Shepherd Leadership

Wisdom for Leaders from Psalm 23

JOSSEY-BASS
A Wiley Imprint
www.josseybass.com

Published by Jossey-Bass
A Wiley Imprint
989 Market Street, San Francisco, CA 94103   www.josseybass.com

Jossey-Bass books and products are available through most bookstores. To contact Jossey-Bass directly, call our Customer Care Department from within the United States at (800) 956-7739 or outside the United States at (317) 572-3986; fax (317) 572-4002.

Jossey-Bass also publishes its books in a variety of electronic formats. Some content that appears in print may not be available in electronic books.

Published in association with Yates & Yates, LLP, Attorneys and Counselors, Orange, California.

Credits appear on pages 147–149.

Library of Congress Cataloging-in-Publication Data
McCormick, Blaine.
  Shepherd leadership : wisdom for leaders from Psalm 23 / Blaine McCormick
and David Davenport. —1st ed.
    p.   cm.
Includes bibliographical references.
  ISBN 0-7879-6633-9 (alk. paper)
  1. Leadership—Religious aspects—Christianity. 2. Bible. O.T. Psalm
XXIII—Criticism, interpretation, etc. I. Davenport, David. II. Title.
  BV4597.53.L43M43 2003
  253—dc21   2003009616

Printed in the United States of America
FIRST EDITION
HB Printing   10 9 8 7 6 5 4

Contents

To our wives, Sarah and Sally,
who are wonderful models of shepherd leadership.

Chapter One

The Shepherd as Leader

The Lord is my shepherd.

There seems to be no end of books for aspiring leaders. Hundreds of new titles hit bookstores each month, and it seems as though one in ten has the word *leadership* somewhere in the title. This torrent of books brings with it at least one bit of good news: It suggests that it's possible to learn how to be a better leader. We hope to help you become a new kind of leader by offering you a new image of leadership—the leader as shepherd.

The modern leader does not lack for leadership images. We've heard the leader described as coach, cheerleader, mentor, artist, cowboy, conductor, guide, explorer, and philosopher, to name just a few. Two of the most popular images of leadership we know seem contradictory: leader as servant and leader as soldier. What gives us the right to add shepherd leader on top of this stack? After all, most people think of shepherds as either gentle young men gird in flowing robes or—worse yet—"Little Bo Peep."

Our confidence in presenting the leader as shepherd is grounded in three observations. First, the general impression of shepherds as gentle people in lush green pastures is inadequate at best and misguided at worst. Shepherds might be gentle, but they're also tough as nails. If you have seen Michelangelo's famous sculpture of David in Florence, you know the Psalmist as a man of great strength.

Second, we think the shepherd image offers a fuller picture of the life of a leader than many others. It's not that these other depictions are necessarily wrong, but we find them incomplete. Third,

1

our image of the shepherd leader is grounded in and inspired by one of the greatest texts of all time: the Twenty-Third Psalm.

Psalm 23 is one of the best-known passages in the Bible. Almost everyone can quote sections of this familiar psalm due to its common usage during times of tragedy and crisis. Psalm 23 has achieved this popularity because it is both a great poem and a sacred text. As great poetry, it gives us the powerful image of a vulnerable sheep protected by a strong, loving shepherd. As a sacred text, it reminds us that there is much beyond ourselves of which to be in awe. Although it is traditionally known as a psalm of comfort, Psalm 23 could also enjoy a very different reputation as a psalm of empowerment for leaders. In fact, we want to show you how to read Psalm 23 as a poem about great leadership written from the perspective of a very satisfied follower.

King David,* one of Israel's greatest leaders, wrote Psalm 23. Before he became king of Israel, however, David was a shepherd. In our modern age, we romanticize shepherding as a calm, peaceful activity. David, however, would have disagreed with this oversimplification. For him, shepherding was a dangerous, demanding, round-the-clock kind of job. Shepherding was also a business, and bad shepherding could ruin a family's welfare if the quality of the sheep's meat, wool, skin, or milk diminished. When viewed from this perspective, David's poem about shepherding might seem more relevant to twenty-first-century business leaders.

With this new outlook in mind, read Psalm 23 again seeking to understand it as a follower reflecting on his or her leader. Although you might know the Psalm quite well, our hope is that you're reading it now as though for the first time. Note the satisfaction in the voice of the follower. Hear the admiration the follower has for the leader. If your followers wrote a poem about you, what would it say?

---

*You will find two Davids populating this book. David, king of Israel, will most often be referred to as "the Psalmist David." David Davenport, past president of Pepperdine University, will be referred to as simply "David."

The LORD is my shepherd, I shall not want.
He maketh me to lie down in green pastures;
He leadeth me beside the still waters;
He restoreth my soul.
He leadeth me in the paths of righteousness for his name's sake.
Yea, though I walk through the valley of the shadow of death,
I will fear no evil, for thou art with me;
Thy rod and thy staff they comfort me.
Thou preparest a table before me in the presence of mine enemies.
Thou anointest my head with oil;
My cup runneth over.
Surely goodness and mercy shall follow me all the days of my life,
And I will dwell in the house of the LORD for ever.

The rest of this book is devoted to exploring the wisdom of this psalm. Every line of this sacred text can unlock new and unexpected insight on the leadership role. Before we do that, we'll give you a clear idea of what makes a shepherd leader different.

Shepherd Leadership in Context

Much of our current leadership thinking and practice is rooted in the Industrial Age, and for good reason. The demands placed on us by the technological innovations fueling the Industrial Age required a new kind of leadership, and management gurus responded splendidly. Pioneering thinkers like Frederick Taylor, father of scientific management, gave America's leaders a task-oriented, machine-centered model, and the resulting productivity leaps were exponential. Administrative innovators like General Motors' Alfred Sloan perfected the multidivisional organization allowing profit-driven companies to achieve unprecedented levels of scale and scope. The new leadership paradigms of the Industrial Age worked wonders for almost three-quarters of a century before cracks started to appear.

Despite increasing levels of both influence and affluence, critics began labeling the leadership spawned by the Industrial Age as "dehumanizing," "mechanistic," and "shortsighted." One of the most influential of these voices was that of Robert Greenleaf. He responded to the problems of the Industrial Age with the idea of servant leadership in his now classic essay "The Servant as Leader." In this and other writings, Greenleaf makes a persuasive case for the necessity of a humane servant leader in building effective organizations and societies. People quickly recognized the wisdom of Greenleaf's writings, and the leader-as-servant image was broadly adopted as a possible cure for the ills of the Industrial Age paradigm.

Greenleaf found insight by turning the hierarchy of the Industrial Age upside down. His achievement should not surprise us since he followed one of the classic creativity techniques: reverse what you're doing and look for insight. For example, instead of asking, "How can we make the best cup of coffee in the world?" ask "How can we make the worst cup of coffee in the world?" Or instead of asking, "How can we decrease our turnover rates?" ask "How can we triple our turnover rates?" He simply asked, "What if someone chose to be a servant first and then to be a leader?"

We agree with much of Greenleaf's insights. Servant leadership started us down an important road, but we believe that servant leadership didn't go far enough. Our own search for inspiration regarding new leadership models involved our reversing the timeline of history rather than the hierarchy of the organization. With Psalm 23 as our guide, we circled back around to the Agrarian Age and found a surprisingly useful model—the leader as shepherd.

In Psalm 23, the leader is a highly visible shepherd who performs the servant's work and then some. Like servants, shepherds care for the needs of their sheep in what often seems to be a one-way relationship. Should the shepherd abdicate the servant role, the flock would quickly fall into trouble, as sheep are not known for their ability to care for their own needs. Sheep need a servant leader to find them food and water, bind their wounds, and even carry them when the going gets tough. Make no mistake, there's plenty of serving in the shepherd role. Yet if shepherds were only servants, the flock would quickly find itself in trouble.

Whereas servant leadership downplays hierarchy and status differences, shepherd leadership places the leader squarely at the front of the followers to serve as a role model. Maggie Lena Walker was born during Reconstruction in 1867 when African American women often found themselves working as household servants. As a member of the first generation of African Americans born into freedom, Walker chose the path of the shepherd leader rather than the role of servant. At age thirty-two, the deeply religious Walker took over an ailing insurance company with $40 in the bank and debts of over $400 and transformed it into a highly successful enterprise with a $70,000 cash reserve and over 100,000 members, mostly minorities.

Before she died in 1934, Walker founded a bank, a newspaper, and a department store—all catering to the African American community in Richmond, Virginia. Her bank provided financing for homes in the black community and loans for minority-owned businesses. A revolutionary accomplishment in her day, the department store was owned by black entrepreneurs, staffed by black employees, and catered to black consumers. As a shepherd leader, Walker visibly stepped out in front, found a better path, and met the needs of her followers, never being so far out in front that she could not come alongside. Like Walker, leaders become shepherds when they awaken to the reality that their actions and decisions can improve the quality of their followers' lives forever.

What Is a Shepherd Leader?

Shepherd leadership is whole-person leadership. It's not just a matter of thinking in a certain way or doing things in a certain way. It's a fully integrated life—a matter of head *and* hand *and* heart. We like to say that it's a way of thinking *and* doing *and* being.

First of all, shepherd leadership is a way of thinking. In the field, sheep are not famous for their strategic planning. As far as we know, animals do not have the capacity to visualize the future. The shepherd's first job in the field is to think and to think ahead. Although humans have this capacity, we know that not everybody uses it. For many people, the concerns of day-to-day survival often override any effort to plan for the future—despite good intentions to the contrary. This is where shepherd leadership enters the picture.

A shepherd leader is somewhat like a good travel guide. The dictionary tells us that a guide assists travel in unfamiliar territory or to an unfamiliar destination by accompanying the traveler. If you have ever enjoyed touring with a great guide, you know what a wonderful and enriching experience it can be. Somehow, without directly trying to control your every move, a good guide nevertheless empowers you to see more and learn more than would ever be possible on your own.

Shepherd leaders are characterized by mental agility. They have the ability to shift gears from deep reflection to quick thinking and decision making in a matter of moments. Most people would agree that good leaders are characterized by both kinds of thinking. Few understand how quickly actual leaders must shift between these two modes. The mind of a shepherd leader must always be out ahead, envisioning the next destination and the best way to get there. There are green fields and dangerous valleys, and the shepherd must anticipate both. In various chapters of this book, we will explore how shepherd leaders lead in right paths, prepare for the worst case, and frame a positive future.

Thinking is something a shepherd leader may often do alone. In contrast, when in the doing mode, the shepherd leader is often with others. In the field, the shepherd is out among the sheep taking care of their needs. Likewise, shepherd leaders are busy doing things for their followers. We see the shepherd leader of Psalm 23 doing something very important for his followers: cultivating abundance. If an ancient shepherd's sheep enjoyed a green pasture, it's because the shepherd had carved it out of the wilderness. Likewise when leaders provide an environment of contentment and abundance, there is far more growth and progress. Shepherd leaders are also out among their followers, assessing and meeting needs. They are managing conflict and removing irritants and obstacles. Wherever there's a shepherd, there's life abundant.

Finally, shepherd leadership is a way of being. In particular, it's a way of "being with" the follower. By "being with" we mean going beyond doing things for the follower or thinking about the follower. A hallmark of shepherd leadership is both the ability and the willingness to see life from the perspective of the follower. Psalm 23 is a powerful demonstration of David's ability to see life from the perspective of a follower.

It would be shortsighted to think of the shepherd-sheep relationship as a one-sided deal for the shepherd. In reality, the shepherd and the sheep had a mutually beneficial relationship. The sheep enjoyed a longer, healthier life under the protection of the shepherd. Likewise, the shepherd enjoyed a longer, healthier life because of the sheep, which provided him with a ready source of warm clothing and relieved him of the obligation to hunt for all of his food. Historians contend that sheep would have long ago become extinct had it not been for their willingness to become domesticated in the care of shepherds. Many ancient civilizations revolved around the relationship between humans and sheep. In those days, sheep were not regarded as "dumb animals" but were held in very high esteem.

Shepherd leaders are distinctive in that while thinking ahead, they are very much "with" the sheep. Shepherding is not a remote form of leadership; it is high touch. Shepherds do not issue a lot of memos and orders from the corner office; rather, they get out in the field to model and guide. Chapters on how shepherd leaders are present with their flock, lead immortals, cultivate loyalty, and become both leader and follower elaborate on this important dimension of leadership.

Chapter Two

Shepherds Meet Needs

I shall not want.
He maketh me to lie down in green pastures;
He leadeth me beside the still waters.

David remembers telling the emergency room doctor that the alpine slide—a plastic sled you ride down a mountain track in summer— had not seemed especially dangerous. "Well," the surgeon replied, "anytime you combine the human body, high speed, and concrete, there is danger. The concrete hasn't lost one yet." Those few moments of family vacation fun in Vermont landed David in a hospital with a broken femur, the largest bone in the body, and gave him several new perspectives on life.

Until the hospital stay and recovery on crutches and canes, David had not realized how "needy" he was. Previously, he had gone through life meeting most of his own needs and often those of others. But a patient in a hospital bed is almost completely dependent on nurses and others to meet his needs. Even out of the hospital, a guy with a stiff and swollen leg is unable to put on his own socks, and with two crutches, it is impossible to carry even a glass of water or a plate of food. Lesson number one, learning to seek and accept help, came hard for a self-sufficient type. David's five-year-old son kindly put socks on Dad's feet every morning, and everyone learned to keep an eye on Dad.

Another lesson was even more instructive. Slowed from his normal breakneck pace, David became more aware of people with physical limitations and special needs. Having to let people meet his needs brought him into some new relationships and, since "the boss" or "Dad" needed help, altered the nature of others. Moving more slowly and empathically through the day made David, in the words of a former president, a kinder, gentler person. He found himself reaching out to others in physical therapy, for example, in an effort to provide encouragement. Although he would not recommend a broken leg to accomplish such improvements, David reports that he liked himself better during that recovery period.

Sheep Are Needy

Like a patient in a hospital or a newborn baby, sheep have needs, most of which they are unable to meet themselves. Although sheep are not known to use alpine slides, they nevertheless have their share of physical problems. On the outside, sheep are attacked by parasites such as ticks, lice, and scabies. Sheep cannot rest when these are present, so they are busy trying to remove them with their mouth or feet or else rubbing against a fence and passing them along to others. Then there are internal parasites: worms in the digestive system or in the throat or lungs or even in the brain. Digestive disorders are not uncommon.

On top of this are what might be called social problems. Although we think of sheep in pleasant, pastoral scenes, conflict within the flock can be a challenge. Far more serious are the wolves and other predators who will attack and enjoy a lamb dinner if given the opportunity. Against these dangers, sheep are defenseless.

Even meeting their daily needs can be a major undertaking. Especially in ancient times, but even today, sheep frequently inhabit dry, barren land. The green pastures one might see in the countryside of England, for example, were not part of the landscape where the Psalmist David shepherded his flock in Israel. Green pastures did not spring up on their own, and still waters were not always at hand. Meeting these needs was part of the work and daily concern of the shepherd.

Against this backdrop of needs, the Psalmist makes a bold and striking statement when he says that under his leader, he does not want. His needs are met. He wants for nothing. This is a kind of double good news, in that he does not experience the pain or restlessness of want and he enjoys the contentedness of fulfillment. As the commercial says, contented cows give more milk! A flock of sheep that eats and rests will be far more profitable than one constantly fighting disease, predators, and hunger.

But the Psalmist goes further. Not only does he not experience want, but two of his greatest needs, food and water, are met in abundance. His leader makes certain that he enjoys green pastures and still waters. To provide green pastures in barren land, the shepherd had to work diligently to clear and prepare the fields. The sheep must be moved constantly because, left unattended, they will overeat in the same places. Furthermore, the sheep must feel entirely free of fear and danger to lie down and enjoy the abundance the shepherd has provided. The picture here is one of fertility, richness, and fullness of life.

Equally, still waters suggest real abundance. Like human beings and other animals, a sheep's body is mostly water and requires replenishment. Much of that can be accomplished by eating the dewy morning grass, but shepherds also built wells for the sheep and tried to locate ponds. Just as they would overeat a good field, sheep would drink dirty water if not supervised. But sheep are naturally afraid of running streams—imagine trying to swim in a wool topcoat and you get the picture—so still waters are the ultimate refreshment. The shepherd leader truly meets the needs of his flock and then some.

Shepherd Leaders Meet Needs

In an earlier day, corporations and other organizations were built around the notion that workers were there to meet the needs of management. While that is still true, of course, wise leaders now understand that they must also meet the needs of their followers. In fact, orienting leaders toward meeting the needs of followers is one of the central features of shepherd leadership.

In studies that could have come right from the sheep pasture, psychologist Abraham Maslow reported that humans have a hierarchy of needs. In his 1954 book *Motivation and Personality*, Maslow points out that for people to move toward their own vision of excellence, or self-actualization, their needs for physical survival must first be met: food, air, sleep, water, and shelter. Then they must feel protected from illness and danger. Next there must be a sense of belonging, through acceptance, affection, and understanding. Near the top comes a need for esteem, pride, self-respect, and status. And finally, once all those needs are met, an individual can reach full potential.

The applications for shepherd leaders are profound indeed. Like the contented cows and the sheep that "shall not want," people will achieve peak performance only when their needs are met. And their needs are not purely economic. People today bring a whole range of needs to the workplace, even beyond those Maslow observed half a century ago.

Surveys have consistently shown that money is not the primary need or motivator prompting excellent performance. A survey by Robert Half International indicated that a lack of praise and recognition was the primary reason people leave their jobs today. Daniel Boyle, vice president and treasurer of Diamond Fiber Products, Inc., told of an employee who paraded her 100 Club jacket, given as special employee recognition, explaining that it was "the first time in the eighteen years I've been there they've recognized the things I do every day." She felt she earned the wages, but the nylon and cotton jacket met her need for recognition. Bob Nelson's books—*1001 Ways to Reward Employees* and *1001 Ways to Energize Employees*—are packed with practical suggestions.

If you visited a Silicon Valley technology company in the hot days of the Internet boom, you would have seen table tennis and pool tables, along with the modern version of green pastures and still waters—a buffet of free food, ranging from soft drinks and candies to breakfast cereal. Of course, sugar and caffeine were not entirely unselfish rewards for those long hours and late nights. Social activities on the company's dollar are routinely expected. People today demand a sense of involvement in, or at least familiarity with, the strategic direction of their organization.

In short, shepherd leaders must learn to conceptualize a great deal of their activity in terms of making sure people's needs are met. Engaging not just people's time but also their minds and hearts is a primary responsibility of the shepherd leader. To do that, the shepherd must keep a close eye on the flock, both day and night, and must unselfishly serve the needs of others. Understanding the organizational value of meeting needs, and reframing the work of leadership in those terms, is the most difficult aspect of this crucial phase of shepherding.

Discovering the Needs

We don't know who discovered water, but it wasn't a fish. How difficult it is for those of us in the midst of organizations to see what people's real needs are. More challenging still is seeing them from the top of the leadership pyramid. As the first President Bush learned painfully on the campaign trail, people are quick to pounce on any sign that a leader is out of touch with the people, in this case questioning whether he knew the price of milk and making much of his surprise at seeing then-common scanners in supermarkets. Of course, the president of the United States cannot hop in the car and drive to the local market for his milk, and there was evidence that his surprise was about the extent, not the existence, of scanner technology, but all this reinforced the view that he was not in touch with the economic challenges confronting ordinary Americans. Bill Clinton's campaign staff, by contrast, had its regular reminder for the 1992 campaign: "It's the economy, stupid."

At the outset, it is valuable to get a handle on the needs within an organization. For one thing, there are individual needs and organizational needs, and they all have to be discovered and met. Another useful distinction is between needs and wants. As the Rolling Stones put it, "You can't always get what you want," and a shepherd leader is not a Santa Claus handing out goodies. Yet another preliminary issue is that different constituencies within an organization—customers, shareholders, executives, clerks, janitors—will have different needs. All of this requires fairly sophisticated approaches to defining and recognizing legitimate needs to be met.

Of course, leadership is people, people, people, and discovering people's needs begins with proactive listening. It must be a reflection of our misplaced priorities that leaders are frequently given special training in public speaking but almost never in listening. And yet the higher you rise in organizational leadership, the less you need to say, because each word is now more powerful, and the more you need to listen to the voices of others. Shepherd leaders must commit considerable time to listening to the flock. Asking them to tell you about their successes, their failures, their challenges, and their problems and then truly listening is both a powerful form of communication and a way to understand their needs.

Shepherd leaders listen in a specific way to ascertain the needs of the flock. Shepherds are up early, checking to see if their sheep survived the night and are healthy to start the day. Then throughout the day, shepherds find various vantage points where they can keep a more or less continuous eye on their flock. Like the parent of a teenager, even at night, shepherds sleep with one eye open and one ear listening. Being alert to the needs of the flock is truly a round-the-clock job.

Listening to the people you lead is listening with a purpose. It is not only to hear the content or substance of what people tell you but also to understand the condition, the morale, of those in your organization. The great prayer of Saint Francis summarizes this kind of listening so well: "Lord grant that I may not seek to be understood as to understand."

If you test yourself, you will find that often when you think you are listening to someone, you are really just catching some of what the person is saying while at the same time formulating what you will say in response. The shepherd leader fights this urge because knowing the condition of the sheep is a profit-and-loss, life-and-death matter. The shepherd leader listens primarily to understand, to hear between the lines, and not to be understood.

Listening, however, is not enough. Just as sheep are not able to communicate their needs directly to the shepherd, people in organizations sometimes do not know what their needs may be and are unable to convey them to leadership. In both organizations David has led, he found it worth the time and expense to undertake a more specific needs assessment, on both an individual and a corporate basis. In every case, he received particularly valuable data that provided insight into deeper needs to be met.

To seek out individual needs, David invited a management psychologist to work with the executive team at first, later delving more deeply into the organization. He administered a test that assessed people's strengths, needs, and stress behaviors. It was a little tricky initially, since folks were uncertain what he might find or how the results would be used. To break the ice, a couple of the high-ranking shepherds went first, allowing the psychologist to share with the others what he had found out about their leaders. The other executives were so intrigued that everyone wanted to participate, and they learned a great deal together. Understanding and respecting different needs and learning how to meet one another's needs more fully laid an important base.

Assessing corporate needs in a formal way is also a must. For one thing, doing so lets the organization know that you care. The aphorism is really true: "I don't care what you know until I know that you care." It is important to do a survey of corporate needs and morale at least every two or three years, comparing the data with what was learned in prior years. Even more important is demonstrating that you are listening by reporting what you have learned and following up in visible ways.

On at least one occasion, David felt it was important to go into a particular department and listen to each member—approximately twenty to twenty-five people—individually at some length. This is an intensive method of needs assessment that cannot be done often, but it provides a powerful experience for both the shepherd leader and the flock. He was able to hear and understand needs of that area in a direct and meaningful way, and it framed the key actions he took as the leader. Once again, the process of listening was almost as important as the content of what he learned.

Meeting the Needs

The psychological profiling David used, known as the Birkman method, shows in several categories how people act in their normal, everyday strengths; what needs they have; and how they respond if their needs are not met. When your needs are met, you are strong and able to perform at a top level. When they are not, you go into stress, exhibiting behaviors you can come to recognize. The goal, of course, is to minimize the stress and to operate from your strengths as much as possible, which is all a function of making sure your needs are met. That pretty well says it all.

It is important to learn to read the stress behaviors of your people, to know when their needs are not met. Some people become very vocal and let you know they have needs; others may retreat into their office and close the door. Either way, you need to understand what that behavior means and try to assess what needs are unmet. Unfortunately, unmet needs are even more powerful motivators than needs that are fulfilled. If left unattended, they can move even the best and most productive people into a long-term negative spiral.

Mary Kay Ash founded her highly successful company on the premise that at the time, there were many women at home who needed part-time work and opportunities for inspiration and recognition. Mary Kay Cosmetics emphasized the creation of a nurturing corporate environment, with lots of prizes, awards, and recognition for success, including her famous pink Cadillacs for the very top performers. Merry Maids discovered that its workforce had special needs, from counsel on how to manage money to simple recognition for birthdays, and meeting those needs has inspired greater loyalty in a high-turnover business.

This is one area where the qualities of a shepherd leader are really quite different from the typical view of leadership. A shepherd is not a driving, pushing kind of leader but rather is characterized more by patience, insight, persistence, diligence, and care. These are precisely the attributes needed by a shepherd leader who will assess and meet the needs of people. It is about being with people, having insight into how they think and feel, patiently observing changes in behavior, and responding appropriately. Do not assume, however, that this kind of work is for the weak. There is a toughness and a strength about shepherds, and qualities like patience, persistence, and diligence are not for the faint of heart.

We have both enjoyed the benefit of bosses who conceptualized their role as helping meet our needs. Being president of a university is a round-the-clock, high-pressure position, and Pepperdine's board did everything possible to meet David's needs and make his work more effective. Likewise, Blaine's superiors at Baylor work creatively to meet his needs for teaching schedules and research funding so that he can excel at both teaching and scholarship. When we feel support, we give far more to our jobs than we ever thought we had to give. It is essentially through these enlightened shepherds that we have seen the value of leadership as meeting needs. When you have followers in whom you have basic trust and confidence, meeting their needs adds fuel to their performance, which is a win for you, for them, and for the organization you serve together.

If, over time, a leader and a follower cannot get in sync and the follower's needs cannot be met, the follower should leave, either voluntarily or by invitation of the boss. A visit with a modern-day shepherd confirmed that a sheep that is consistently unhappy or disaffected has a negative impact on the shepherd and the rest of the flock and should be given a chance to find happiness elsewhere. In almost every case, such a move is best for the sheep as well as for the shepherd and flock that is left behind.

In a way, it is quite remarkable that the Psalmist David, who had been through many difficult times, could make such a strong statement: I shall not want. He had been on the run from his predecessor, Saul, and even from his son Absalom. To some degree, his perspective reflects the frame of mind of a contented follower. But it also reveals one of the most important characteristics of the shepherd leader: the ability to frame the leadership process as energizing people by meeting their fundamental needs.

Shepherd Thinking

🖢 How do you feel when you think about conceptualizing leadership as meeting needs? Resentful? Empowered? Burdened? This is a place to start.

🖢 To what degree have you made formal attempts to assess the needs of individuals under your leadership or of the entire organization that you lead?

🖢 What might it feel like to be so contented that you could say, "I do not want"? What might it take professionally for you to get there?

Shepherd Doing

🖢 Ask two or three people how well their needs are being met by you and the organization. Listen proactively and fully to their responses.

🖢 List what you perceive your own professional needs to be. Share them with a spouse or close colleague to sharpen your understanding of needs and to learn to share at that level.

🖢 Rank yourself as a listener on a scale of 1 to 10. Ask some colleagues to rank you and compare.

Chapter Three

Shepherds Lead Immortals

He restoreth my soul.

Oskar Schindler captures both the greatness and complexity of shepherd leadership. You probably know Schindler as the center of the book and film *Schindler's List*. During World War II, Schindler successfully shepherded more than a thousand Jews through one of the darkest valleys in world history using a rather unexpected strategy: he employed them as workers in his factories. With his actions, Schindler showed us how business can be transformed from a product-making activity into a life-giving activity.

Schindler exemplified the courage, initiative, and goodness that are essential to shepherd leadership. He honored his Jewish workers in a variety of ways—often at great personal risk. He created safe corners in his factory where the rabbis could usher in the Sabbath and allowed workers to bake Passover matzohs in the factory ovens. He set aside decent burial grounds for the Jews who died from illnesses while in his care. Another time, he gratefully kissed one of his Jewish workers who presented a gift to him—an affirmation of humanity in almost every culture. Nonetheless, Schindler was arrested and nearly thrown in jail for simply being humane to the untouchables of his day. Unlike his Nazi counterparts, Schindler treated his Jewish workers as soul-bearing humans rather than animals. Nobody was beaten or murdered in his factories.

Schindler is a perfect example of a shepherd who stayed true to the rightness of his actions rather than worried about his short-term results. After all, his compassion paid poor dividends for those interested solely in monetary returns. Schindler's businesses helped him become a rich man during the war, but he was penniless when Germany surrendered as the costs of keeping his Jewish workers safe mounted. Furthermore, his story stayed on the margin of obscurity for decades until one persistent Jewish survivor finally got the attention of an author and, later, a film director. Before Oskar Schindler died, he was honored as a "Righteous Person" and invited to plant a tree on the "Avenue of the Righteous" at the Yad Vashem museum in Jerusalem.

Why One Sheep Matters

Not only do sheep need shepherds to protect them from predators, but they also need shepherds to fix boundaries that keep them from wandering away. Despite a strong herding instinct, renegade sheep somehow bent on self-destruction have been known to lose the rest of the flock. The familiar images of lost sheep and searching shepherds testify to the fact that sheep are capable of overcoming their herding instinct, the shepherd's boundaries, and their own survival instinct . . . and simply wander off.

So why would a shepherd leave the entire flock and go searching for a single sheep that was dumb enough to wander off in the first place? From a cost-benefit standpoint, seeking out lost sheep seems to make no economic sense whatsoever. Just cut your losses, shore up your boundaries, and move on. Why endanger the rest of the flock with your absence?

First of all, shepherding was a high-touch activity, and the good shepherd had a name for every one of his sheep. Usually, this name described something unique about the sheep. Some names like "Big Boy" or "Little One" referred to the size of the sheep. Other names like "Hop-Along" or "One Ear" were rooted in something abnormal about the sheep. Still others like "Scruffy" or "Feisty" were rooted in the unique personality traits a sheep might possess. It's pretty clear that the sheep were more than just com-modities to the shepherd.

Second, that errant sheep might be somewhere you don't want it to be. When Keith Lynch loses a sheep, he could get a call from the Secret Service. That's because Lynch's sheep ranch is very close to President Bush's Prairie Chapel Ranch in Crawford, Texas. "It's just natural for a sheep to go through a hole in the fence," Lynch told us. We always pictured lost sheep as wandering around some-where in the wilderness, but Lynch's story suggests that lost sheep are often on somebody else's property. And when that somebody else's property is guarded by the Secret Service, one hopes that the lost sheep isn't over there getting into things it shouldn't. "You gotta be neighborly about the lost sheep," Lynch taught us with a wry smile.

Working with Immortals

C. S. Lewis observed in his essay "The Weight of Glory," "There are no *ordinary* people. You have never talked to a mere mortal. Nations, cultures, arts, civilizations—these are mortal, and their life is to ours as the life of a gnat. But it is immortals whom we joke with, work with, marry, snub, and exploit. . . . Next to the Blessed Sacrament itself, your neighbor is the holiest object presented to your senses."

To be a shepherd is to be awakened to the reality that you work among immortals. The eminent British social critic George Orwell contended that the widespread loss of belief in immortality has done more damage to modern life than anything else. Without souls, people become commodities to be bought and sold like any other animal. With souls, people become unique, majestic creations that cannot be used and discarded without consequence. This is probably what happened with Oskar Schindler. He began the war as an opportunist hoping to make some easy money off the cheap labor the Jews offered. Somewhere along the way, however, he awakened to the immortals in his workplace and started treating his workers like divine creations.

As with Schindler, shepherd leadership is about learning to view oneself and others through the lens of an immortal soul. This is difficult because we have a "church on Sunday, work on Monday" attitude that compartmentalizes material and spiritual matters. More than one person with whom we spoke while writing this book talked of the challenge of maintaining a people focus in the task-focused world of business. As one manager told us, "I really don't care if they're sick. My concern is about who is going to take care of the station." In the same breath, though, the manager admitted that this attitude is shortsighted because he cares deeply about his followers.

Seeing the immortal soul within another doesn't necessarily make a tough situation any less difficult. It only brings into focus one of the many paradoxes that shepherd leaders face: We live in a material world and a spiritual world at the same time. Awareness of this paradox will lead to a certain tension in our leadership motives and actions. Best of all, seeing the soul within others doesn't restrict our alternatives. Rather, it opens up an even broader range of possible responses that we might overlook if we lose sight of the soul.

To believe that we work among created beings with eternal destinies changes how we might interact with people in moments of conflict or moments of temptation. As shown in the illustration, see the humans in the following scenarios through the lens of an immortal soul and consider how that changes the dynamics of the situation.

- A difficult customer constantly points out faults in your products in order to justify discounts. The tables turn suddenly when this customer accidentally backs his or her car into part of your building when visiting your business.

- An attractive coworker has responded openly to your flirtatious comments. Both of you are experiencing difficulties in your marriages. You take a business trip with this person, and an affair seems like a real possibility.

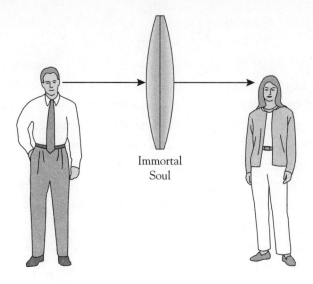

Immortal
Soul

- Your sales manager left two years ago to start a business that competes directly with you. This person shamelessly wooed customers away with big promises and more than a few rumors about you. But his company crumbled, and much to your amazement, he comes to you asking for an entry-level sales job.

- A tough competitor blasts you in the press, spreading vicious rumors about your company. Although there's some merit to the stories, they are blown out of proportion, and you are needlessly vilified, maybe even slandered. When a fire unexpectedly consumes this competitor's office complex, the local newspaper calls you for a comment.

In difficult moments like these, a soul humanizes an individual we might otherwise stereotype as an enemy. Even if this person has caused us intentional harm, we can still choose to treat the person with justice rather than vengeance. Beyond this, forgiveness, reconciliation, and compassion—though difficult—become genuine possibilities in light of shared eternal destinies.

Leading with Soul

Leaders who intentionally view life and followers through the lens of immortality do a better job of creating workplaces that nourish both the material and spiritual sides of life. One of Blaine's friends is the manager of a Chili's restaurant in Waco, Texas. Scott's parent company constantly measures him on a number of financial and performance metrics. At the same time, Scott personally chooses to stay focused on two soul-honoring principles: celebration and hospitality. At which restaurant would you rather dine? At one where they're motivated by profit only or at one where they're motivated by profit, celebration, and hospitality? Critics might claim that these are mutually exclusive, but Scott is convinced that "when I keep focused on celebration and hospitality, the profits will follow." He is clearly viewing life through a different lens.

Chick-fil-A founder Truett Cathy has proved adept at keeping soul at the center of one of the nation's largest fast-food chains. Not only does the company maintain an aggressive program of corporate philanthropy, but it also has the distinction of being the only national restaurant chain that doesn't open on Sundays. Rooted in the Cathy family's Christianity, the practice allows restaurant managers and employees to spend a full day away from work with their families or in personal pursuits. Chick-fil-A enjoys two great benefits from this policy. First, it manages to attract the same amount of business in six days that its competitors do in seven. Second, Chick-fil-A may have the lowest turnover rates of any nationwide fast-food restaurant: 5 to 25 percent, in an industry that can easily top 300 percent turnover in a bad year.

Shepherd leaders don't necessarily have to dismantle a bureaucracy. Rather, they just have to acknowledge the humanity that populates the bureaucracy. For example, a bureaucracy sends a death certificate and prints an obituary. A shepherd acknowledges the pain of loss and finds a way to help. When David called his college professors to tell them he would need to be away for awhile because of the sudden death of his father, one teacher broke through the bureaucracy and reached out to him on a human level. Learning that David had no car and no way home, Professor Mosier told David to pack his things and be in front of his dorm in thirty minutes. The professor picked him up, took him to his travel agent to get a plane ticket, and drove him to the airport. That was an act of kindness by a Stanford professor David will never forget.

Shepherds Restore Gifts to the Community

Shepherds know that each sheep brings something unique to the herd. Better still, two sheep's gifts might complement one another so that one plus one might not equal two but even three, four, or five. A good example of this are prized ewes that always bear twins or triplets. A sheep is not just an asset to a shepherd. Rather, each is a unique creation that needs to be brought back to the flock rather than abandoned when straying.

The Jewish Talmud states, "Whoever saves a single soul, it is as if he had saved the entire world." Wisdom like this turns cost-benefit analysis on its head by suggesting that there's more contained within one individual than meets the observer's eye. Shepherd leadership is about seeing each one of your followers as a unique creation with gifts capable of serving others in the community. Sometimes the shepherd leader's job is to get the right gifts in the right place—like helping a gifted young musician obtain a scholarship to a top music school. At other times, the shepherd leader is called to rescue people from themselves and restore their gifts to the larger community.

Most people would agree that Al Pacino is a gifted actor. Who among us has not marveled at his work in films like *Scent of a Woman, The Insider,* or the *Godfather* trilogy? Yet these gifts were almost lost to the world but for a shepherd who could see beyond some bad habits. After a string of successful films in the early 1970s, Pacino was living large and enjoying his fame. He met a close friend at a restaurant one day and began another round of what had become a regular habit of heavy drinking. After some initial banter and some invitations to join the fun, Pacino's friend looked him squarely in the eye and said, "Al, please. Just be aware of what you're doing."

Pacino later called this brief interaction a turning point in his life. He believes it saved him from a life of alcohol abuse. And who was this friend? A minister? A social worker? A family member? None of the above. Rather, it was his manager and agent, Charlie. Making the world a better place is not limited to the role of minister, activist, or social worker but extends to the business leader as well. Unfortunately, many business leaders fumble away incredible opportunities because they think it's out of their domain. Pacino's friend Charlie didn't try to call a minister into the situation. Rather, he stepped up and ministered in his role as agent and manager. We'll be the first to say that businesses exist to make money. As such, they can't operate like social agencies, attempting to rescue every broken person who enters the door. If they did, they probably wouldn't be able to stay in business for very long. Nevertheless, as Pacino's agent demonstrated, there are ways to courageously and compassionately address a variety of individual problems in the workplace.

Every immortal has been given a gift for the community. The shepherd leader's role is to ensure that each and every gift is used by the community. As in Pacino's case, sometimes the community loses a gift because the follower starts to self-destruct. At other times, the community wrongly chooses to exclude the gifts of an entire segment of the population due to racist or sexist attitudes. The response of the shepherd leader is the same in both cases: intentional and decisive action to restore the gifts to the community.

Shepherds Create a Place for Second Chances

It's hip to talk about "failing your way to success," but let's be honest: failure can be pretty humiliating. Take the simple matter of applying for a promotion and not making it. It's especially humiliating when the promotion is a job that somebody else at the company gets and you're passed over. In other words, you failed, and you failed in a very public way. Shepherd leaders watch out for failure and look for ways to restore the souls of those who fail. After all, failure really can be a launching point to other successes; it's just hard to believe that unless somebody reminds you.

Thomas Edison filed an impressive 1,093 patents with the U.S. Patent Office, and behind each one of those 1,093 successes lays hundreds and sometimes thousands of failures. Edison mastered the art of recovering from failure with lessons in hand and sought to pass it on to his workers. Near the end of his career, a former worker, Alfred Tate, penned the following letter to his former boss: "Above all you taught me not to be afraid of failure; that scars are sometimes as honorable as medals."

Most college professors are happy to correspond with their top-performing students. In contrast, a college professor we know has the extraordinary habit of writing to the students who fail his classes. The letter is not a chastising note from a harsh taskmaster. Rather, it's both an apology and an invitation. Instead of laying all the blame on the student, this professor acknowledges his part in the failure and apologizes for letting the student down. Next, rather than running the student off to another class, the professor invites the student to take the course once again with hopes of a better outcome.

A manager we know takes much the same approach with missed promotions. When an employee misses a promotion, he's quick to go directly to the employee and thank the person for having the courage to step forward for greater responsibility. This manager also encourages the employee to keep trying and pledges to keep on the lookout for new opportunities that might fit the employee's abilities and desires. We all, like sheep, stumble and fall in both personal and professional ways. To be a shepherd is to create a space where failure is not fatal.

Before its implosion, Enron was a highly competitive, performance-based organization in which the lowest-performing 10 to 15 percent of employees were fired annually. The pressure to succeed was almost as strong as the pressure not to fail. We say "almost as strong" because the pressure not to fail overrides everything for loss-averse humans. Remember, winning isn't everything in America; it's the only thing. Some people made some pretty big bets at Enron, and when the deals didn't come through, they hid them away in the now infamous SPEs—"special-purpose entities."

When people can't fail, they just roll the bets forward one more quarter or hide them so deep they can't be found. One person can do this and get away with it, but when everyone does it, the whole charade will ultimately fall like a house of cards. Interestingly enough, some writers have argued that if Enron had just acknowledged the losses rather than just rolling them forward or hiding them, the company would most likely have survived. Sure, Enron would have had one or two less than stellar years, but the company would still exist, and its name would not be synonymous with scandal.

Shepherd leaders can create second chances for people both inside and outside their firm. Job seekers with criminal records and chemical dependencies are continually plagued by their past. Even if they come clean, businesses are hesitant to hire them when they discover the criminal convictions or drug-testing records from their past. Often they just need one employer to take a chance on them so they can provide evidence of their ability to be a good worker. More often than not, however, this chance never comes.

In 1979, John D. Beckett and Ed Seabold created a way for a number of these workers to use their gifts once again in the workplace. Beckett and Seabold started Advent Industries, a for-profit business that subcontracts work for Beckett's own company, the R. W. Beckett Corporation, the nation's largest manufacturer of residential oil burners. The men's goal was to build a company where people with troubled pasts could build a temporary-work record on the way to finding permanent employment. Advent employed more than one thousand people between 1979 and 1998. Some washed out immediately, unable to handle the discipline of a regular job. Others, however, stayed in their work programs for periods ranging from six months to two years. This successful work record allowed them to signal to other employers that they were not high-risk hires. Many Advent alumni have gone on to successful jobs and done so with a sense of rightness and purpose that they might not otherwise have had.

To be a shepherd requires a bold living out of both mercy and compassion. Choosing mercy means choosing not to punish an individual when justice demands punishment. Choosing compassion means providing for someone when justice demands that they not receive anything. Shepherd leaders can do this because they've been awakened to the mercy and compassion they have been shown. The Psalmist David's life and leadership was racked with difficulty and shortcomings—betrayal, rebellion, adultery, murder, the deaths of his own children. Despite all of his failures and fallenness, he's still known today as "the man after God's own heart." That's because he saw his own humanity in his failings and left a legacy that encouraged others in the midst of theirs. We've certainly found encouragement in his most famous writing.

Shepherd Thinking

🖝 How does the idea of an eternal soul affect the way I interact with my followers? My customers? My assistant? The coworker with whom I can't bear to work?

🖝 Am I a person who keeps emotions out of the workplace or who acknowledges their presence? Do I find myself enjoying the sterile nature of the bureaucracy?

🖝 How do I want to be shepherded when I fail?

Shepherd Doing

🖝 Try to see your followers in the largest context possible. One suggestion might be to collect pictures of your followers with their families. This might help you understand that your decisions have a broad impact. Furthermore, it sends a strong signal of caring to the follower.

🖙 Honor the souls of all people with whom you interact by calling them by their name and using "sir" or "ma'am" whenever possible. Practice this when you order fast food, go to the video store, check out at the grocery store, and within your own organization. Few things honor a person more than being told "Thank you, ma'am" or "Thank you, Ray."

🖙 In addition to praising people when they do something right, intentionally look for people suffering from failure. Commit yourself to coming alongside that person and shepherding the person back from their failure.

🖙 Review the system of rewards and punishments within your company to see if either is extreme. Both extreme rewards and extreme punishments can motivate people to hide their failures rather than bring them out into the open.

Chapter Four

Shepherds Lead on Right Paths

He leadeth me in the paths of righteousness for
his name's sake.

At some time in childhood, most kids aspire to be a cowboy or cowgirl. Perhaps this explains the popularity of the movie *City Slickers,* in which Billy Crystal and his buddies leave home, job, and family for a vacation on the range, driving cattle. It turns out that moving cows from point A to point B is anything but a vacation, and the men return home sorer but wiser from the experience.

Cowboy imagery, a romantic vision of youth that some people never outgrow, clashes with the art of modern leadership. Watching your leader charge you at full speed on a horse may motivate cows, but it won't work more than, say, once with people. The equipment of a cowboy—spurs, prods, whips, ropes, cutting horses—is not the right tool kit for the modern leader. Even the vocabulary of cowboy leadership—driving the herd—is all wrong with people.

In fact, today you will sometimes hear leaders say that their work is more like herding cats. Perhaps a cat does, in many ways, reflect the greater independence that people expect today in the workplace, at play, or in the family. We watch with a mixture of pain and amusement as old-school coaches try to lead today's young athletes, with their very different ideas about authority and team play. The great baseball manager Leo Durocher's explanation of his retirement sounds like a man who learned that herding ballplayers was no longer in style. He said he was stepping down because "'Sit down! Shut up! Listen!' won't work anymore."

Shepherds Lead in Right Paths

By contrast, the shepherd leader of Psalm 23 is not about the business of herding cats, cattle, or even sheep. The Psalmist David acknowledges a very different style of leadership when he writes, "He leadeth me in the paths of righteousness for his name's sake." This small descriptive phrase contains two of the fundamental elements of shepherd leadership. First, sheep—and people—are led from the front, not herded from behind. We, like sheep, prefer to be drawn, not driven. And second, even in times of change and chaos, and with modern followers who are more independent, leadership is still about finding the right paths to be followed.

Two novice shepherds learned about leading, and not driving, sheep the hard way. Ron and Teresa Parker, city folks from Los Angeles and Wichita, respectively, decided to move to Minnesota and raise sheep. When Garrison Keillor of the *Prairie Home Companion* stopped by their place for a visit, the Parkers shared one of their early lessons: "At first we tried to drive the sheep, . . . running at them and clapping our hands and barking like we imagined sheepdogs bark—and we just about ran ourselves silly. The sheep would move a little ways, turn around, and stare at us. Finally we discovered that sheep can be led. They're out there wandering around and looking for a leader."

What a wonderful parable of modern leadership!

It was also the Psalmist's experience as a shepherd of old that sheep are looking for someone who will lead them. At the beginning of the day, the shepherd gives a morning call, with a voice and a sound that the sheep come to recognize. And with this, he leads them to the feeding grounds, where they will enjoy their breakfast. It is quite amazing that sheep know the voice of their shepherd and will respond to it while ignoring the voices of others. Flocks that have intermingled overnight will separate in the morning as each follows the call of its own shepherd. Recent research by British scientists concludes that sheep even come to recognize and remember as many as fifty different faces, primarily of fellow sheep but also of people.

The Shepherd's Voice

Shepherd leadership does not depend so much on the tools of management as on the relationship between the leader and the led. Unlike the cattle driver, the shepherd employs tools that are relational. In place of hard charging comes familiarity, even intimacy. Instead of prods and whips there are voices and calls. All of this becomes more effective over time as familiarity breeds not contempt but a healthy leader-follower relationship.

If you are to be a shepherd leader, ask yourself whether you are a driver or a leader. Are you able to draw people with your leadership, or do they feel driven? In a small setting, of course, one can truly come to know those you are leading on a personal level, as shepherds would their sheep. Even in larger organizations, however, there are still ways to draw and lead.

One of the primary tools for leading a large flock is communication, both oral and written. Make certain that there are regular opportunities for people to hear your voice, first by making regular presentations, at least monthly, to all your key people. Second, get out of your office and away from the computer for both planned visits to operational areas and unplanned walking around each week. Showing up when and where you are not expected, interacting with the flock on their own terms, is powerful leadership. Finally, walk away from the computer a little bit every day, and deliver some of those messages by phone or in person, where the recipients can hear your voice. Communication for leaders is not just about the content; it's also about the tone and the voice.

Another way to shepherd a large organization is by example, with those in your immediate flock. If there are hundreds or thousands in your company, you can model shepherd leadership with those who work directly with you. Let them spend enough time with you to know your voice, to sense your values and direction, and help them understand that, in turn, you expect them to model this kind of leadership with those in their flock. Law dean Willard Pedrick said that law students learn how to treat their clients by observing how their professors treat them. If you do it well and communicate your expectations, this kind of trickle-down shepherd leadership can be effective.

What the Parkers learned as new shepherds is often true with people: they are just waiting for someone to step out and lead. It doesn't always take a lot of exhorting; often the leader can just go. When Katharine Graham was publisher of the *Washington Post* newspaper, social circles separated the men, who stayed at the table after dinner to discuss politics and affairs of the day, and the women, who retired to another room to talk about family and social things. As a result of her work, Graham spent all day in politics and business and resented being excluded from the male conversation. Rather than giving a speech about it, however, she simply told her host one evening that she would be leaving when the women were excused from the table. The host could not abide her departure, however, and convinced her to stay if he would keep everyone together. Soon this was happening all over town. Quietly, by just going where she felt she should, Graham had initiated a revolution at the dinner tables in our nation's capital.

Get Your Lead Sheep Moving

In a classic *Harvard Business Review* article, "In Praise of Followers," Robert Kelley identified five types of followers: effective followers, yes people, survivors, alienated followers, and sheep. In Kelley's matrix, effective followers are characterized as both active and critical thinkers. By contrast, sheep are described as passive and uncritical thinkers. This conceptualization conforms nicely to the definition of *sheep* from a current dictionary of slang: "someone who follows trends, trying to do what's 'in' or 'popular.'"

Although they may conform to popular notions about sheep, such views don't hold up to anyone who has spent time with real sheep. A variety of personalities exist in a flock, including weak sheep and lead sheep. Any shepherd knows that the most effective way to move a flock is to get your lead sheep moving, since 90 percent of the flock takes its cue from the lead sheep.

The same phenomenon occurs in organizations. Shepherd leaders, by definition, are out in front calling to their followers, and they can maximize their impact by connecting first with those in the organization that are their "lead sheep." Before stepping out, the shepherd leader may wish to sit down with these influential people and both share and sharpen the vision with feedback. By building commitment within the 10 percent who are influence leaders, the shepherd leader gains influence with most of the other 90 percent who take their cues from these influence leaders. Especially in anti-authoritarian cultures like America, people are more likely to respond to their peers than a superior. As persuasion expert Robert Cialdini says, "Influence is best exerted horizontally rather than vertically."

Leading in Right Paths

The Psalmist also said that shepherds lead in right paths. No organization or individual wants to end up like the man who spent his whole life trying to climb the ladder of success, only to find that it was leaning against the wrong wall. Finding the right paths—whether the path to profitability, the path to greater service, or the path to higher ethical and moral ground—is the responsibility of the shepherd leader. Without the paths to green pastures and quiet waters, the sheep will not prosper and may not survive. Or as that great philosopher Yogi Berra put it: "You got to be careful if you don't know where you're going because you might not get there."

Do not assume that because people like flexibility and freedom, they do not value being led in right paths. It is true that terms like *authority* and *boundaries* are not as popular today as they might have been in an earlier time. Compounding the challenge is the fact that most organizations, from companies to families, are traveling paths of greater uncertainty, and sometimes even chaos, than ever before. Finding the paths through the overwhelming data and choices available, however, is also more important than ever before.

If patience was the great virtue of the Agrarian Age and efficiency of the Industrial Age, perhaps making good choices will be the most important quality in the Information Age. Picture the transition from the long silences and lengthy journeys of the agrarian, shepherd world to the speed and efficiency of the factories of the industrial world. Now imagine moving from the highly structured and defined world of industrial production to the flood of information and choices of the Information Age, and you see one of the big challenges of leadership today. In place of the three television networks broadcast over the airwaves and the three flavors of ice cream of an earlier generation, we have three hundred networks delivered via satellite dishes and scores of flavors, even create-your-own. When you access the Internet at any moment today, you have at your command more knowledge and information than anyone who lived before you had in a lifetime. Finding right paths in the Information Age demands that shepherd leaders help their followers make good choices by understanding and framing the options before them.

Another big difference for leaders today is that they are generally most effective when they involve the people in some meaningful way in finding the paths. Sometimes it is as simple as the leader sharing his or her vision and listening to feedback and then sharpening and bringing the vision into focus. At other times, the leader may be most effective in framing the choices and guiding the group toward good decisions. Occasionally, it may be important to seek broad input on the front end of an undertaking. It's not just in baseball that "Sit down, shut up, and listen" is history—it doesn't really work anywhere today.

The beauty of shepherd leadership is that it fits the current non-hierarchical culture so nicely. Most leaders acknowledge that one of their greatest challenges is that they have greater responsibility than they have authority. There is much to do but insufficient power or resources to get it done. Leading without authority is the perfect environment for the shepherd leader. The shepherd leader gently but clearly sets boundaries and outlines the path, exhorting people to go. When they learn to trust and know his voice, they will follow in right paths.

The Leader Must Be on the Right Path

Shepherd leaders must themselves honor boundaries and follow right paths. Once again, the image of the cowboy, so engrained in American culture, works to our detriment. Corporate names like Enron, WorldCom, and Arthur Andersen have come to represent a culture in which cowboy leaders felt free to go their own way, unconstrained by legal and ethical boundaries or by right paths. The specter of major national companies and accounting firms declaring bankruptcy and closing down for failing to follow right paths is now a part of our business history.

Pepperdine M.B.A. students are offered a seminar on the importance of leaders' staying on track when they visit a federal prison for white-collar criminals. There the real estate developer who set up a bank that engaged in self-dealing, the stock broker who moved money improperly in trading, and the corporate embezzler describe where the lines are and how they crossed them. First, of course, they got too close to the line in their daily work. Then came the big day when, just once, they told themselves, it was necessary to cross the line. Soon, before anyone discovered the problem, they felt they could make it right. But then things did not go as planned and they had to cross the line again and again until finally they were caught. All of us in the audience were captivated by these painful stories of leaders who had left the right path. And the advice was clear: you cannot let yourself as a leader leave the right path, because it leads to a different world from which you may never be able to return.

The Rhythm of Shepherd Leadership

One of the greatest challenges for a shepherd leader is finding the
right balance of being out ahead searching for the right paths and
remaining back with the flock, letting your voice be heard as you
lead along the way. To some degree, the emphasis for a particular
leader will depend on his or her own gifts and interests. And over
time, organizational needs will vary. Some research indicates that
leaders often begin their work with a period of intensive listening
but, as the years pass, move toward outside activities and conceptual tasks, where there is less conflict and more stimulating new
ideas. Eventually they lose touch with the flock, their internal support erodes, and they become less effective as leaders.

In an insightful passage on leadership, historian Theodore
White assessed the U.S. presidential campaign of 1964 in just those
terms. In the introduction to *The Making of the President 1964*,
White compared presidential campaigns and leadership to the great
pioneers and wagon trains of the American West. At the end of an
arduous day of travel, the people down in the valley were nursing
their wounds and resting their tired bodies. Up ahead, the leaders
would ascend the next mountain to find the safest and best paths
for tomorrow's travel.

Barry Goldwater was effective on the mountain, seeing the
future and understanding the paths, but not so good down in
the valley communicating his message. Many of Goldwater's perspectives, especially about social security and nuclear weapons,
frightened people at the time but turned out to be relatively accu-
rate. Lyndon Johnson, by contrast, was a master of the valley, feeling people's pain, healing their wounds, and addressing their needs.
At one campaign stop, Johnson seized a bullhorn and shouted,
"We're in favor of a lot of things, and we're against mighty few."
The candidate who could communicate with the sheep overwhelmed the one who was out ahead studying the paths.

In reality, the good shepherd leader must master both the
mountain and the valley, being able to find the right paths and lead

people along them. Indeed, the truly great leaders essentially live in a constant rhythm between time on the mountain and time in the valley. David and his Old Testament peers certainly did this. Moses, for example, would literally climb to the top of the mountain to meet with God and receive his commands and would then descend to the valley to communicate them with the people. David, the great Psalmist, was clearly a man who knew the mountain of reflection, but also as a shepherd king who led his people.

Many leaders candidly admit that this is the most difficult element of their task. It is arduous work to climb the next hill and get a concept of the direction that must be traveled. It takes excellent information, keen intellect to sort through the options, and courage to make the best choice. This can be very lonely work, especially holding the responsibility for the final decisions about the best path.

Now, having wrestled that momentous decision to the ground, comes the difficult task of going back to the valley and sharing it with those who must follow you along that path. Like sheep, they often prefer to go their own way. Some of them will be tired or wounded and not want to travel any path. Still others are obstinate and will resist your path merely because someone in authority chose it. Sharing that decision in the valley is every bit as exhausting and difficult as making it up on the mountaintop.

But there's more. It is almost never sufficient simply to announce the path to everyone one time. No, in a seemingly never-ending pattern, you have to keep sharing the path over and over. Just as the shepherd does not make an announcement or send a memo to the flock, you must lead a few sheep up the trail, and then you have to go back and gather up some more. One frequent lament of leaders is that they feel like they are saying the same things over and over in their communication. And the truth is, they probably are. You feel the energy drain out of you every time you must go back down to the valley, share the message, and lead another group up the mountain. There are times when you feel you absolutely cannot make that voyage even one more time. But leading folks along the right paths is highly personal business, and there is no substitute for the shepherd leader making many trips from the mountain to the valley and back again. It is, in many ways, the most difficult element of leadership, but as we sometimes joke in running academic and nonprofit organizations, that's why they pay us leaders the big bucks! In the end, nothing you do in leadership will matter more than leading people in right paths.

Shepherd Thinking

🐏 Would people characterize you as out in front leading or coming at them driving?

🐏 Look inside your leadership toolbox and list what you see. Are they the tools of a cowboy or a shepherd?

🐏 How often do you spend each day walking the fields, letting people hear your voice?

🐏 Think creatively about your schedule. Is there a way for you to spend some time each month up on the mountain finding new paths? And some time each week down in the valley letting folks hear your voice?

Shepherd Doing

🐏 Set a goal that tomorrow, or next week, you will visit two or three operational areas or two or three key people out in the field, where they work.

🐏 Select several messages you would normally send via e-mail, and go deliver them personally or by phone, allowing people to hear and know your voice.

🐏 Decide on two or three key choices your organization must make, and start talking with people about how to frame the options and make good choices.

Chapter Five

Shepherds Know the Valley

Yea, though I walk through the valley of the
shadow of death . . .

Though we may wish otherwise, we know that life is not all green
pastures and still waters. All of us suffer through periods in dry, barren places, wondering whether we will ever find a way out. Our
friend Lynn Anderson captured how many would have to reword
this psalm in his "Un-Psalm 23":

*I am a sheep without a shepherd. I do not know whom to follow—
and I am utterly in want.*

*I am empty. Nothing satisfies. Nothing refreshes me. I find no real
fulfillment. No lasting security. No real rest.*

I feel like a lost soul—totally, irretrievably depleted.

*I don't believe anyone walks with me in the darkest valley! And
contemplation of my own mortality holds me "all my lifetime in
bondage under fear of death"—for in that final hour I will be
profoundly alone!*

*I feel misguided and I find no authentic comfort in anything.
None.*

*I feel unwelcome in my world, always hungry for something—and
totally overwhelmed by a thousand threatening forces.*

*My blistered head aches, with no oil of relief. My joy cup is dry
all the way to the bottom. Bone dry.*

*I have given up hoping for any real quality to my life. In fact,
genuine goodness and mercy have eluded me all of my days—
and I don't really expect things to change.*

Oh how I ache to belong somewhere. But I don't really feel at home anywhere . . . And I think I will feel lonely and homeless forever.

The Valley

It is impossible to talk about the terrain of life without honestly acknowledging that there are valleys as well as mountaintops. When the Psalmist David is in the valley, however, he is quick to note the comforting role of the shepherd: "Yea, though I walk through the valley of the shadow of death, I shall fear no evil, for thou art with me." At the heart of this remarkable statement, often quoted at funerals and memorial services, lies the spiritual notion of the shepherd as a comforter and protector. Even when facing adversity, David finds his shepherd there with him, in his corner.

Inevitably, sheep traverse valleys, as well as craggy mountains and green pastures, and the shepherd's protection and leadership are all-terrain necessities. Just as the sheep will be led up treacherous mountain paths in the heat of summer to find lush meadows, when cold weather approaches, they must be led back down those dangerous trails into the valley. This is part of the natural rhythm of the life of a sheep. Likewise we all know that in every aspect of life there will be valleys as well as peaks, downs as well as ups. Mountaintop experiences exhilarate us, but they are often followed by valleys of despair that leave us discouraged and possibly depressed.

Using the Valley

Do people develop and grow more in response to success or failure? The answer is both painful and clear: failure is a better teacher than success. Experts in almost every field teach that you can learn far more from failure than from success. Typical is the experience of acclaimed basketball coach Rick Pitino, who admitted, "Everything

I've learned about coaching I've learned from making mistakes." Often it is only when we have been humbled, when life takes us to our knees, that we are truly ready to listen and learn.

If the valley is a better classroom than the mountaintop, it is important, then, not to rush through its curriculum. The valley is a place of testing, forcing us to examine the priorities and values of life. It is a place of solitude, even loneliness, away from the crowds that so often influence our lives and decisions. In contrast to the speedboats we often race across the surfaces of life, the valley challenges us to be more like ocean liners, moving more slowly through deeper waters.

So when you find yourself in the valley, do not assume that your first priority is to escape as quickly as possible. Sometimes it's useful to allow yourself to feel the pain that took you there, in all its intensity. George Pepperdine, the founder of Western Auto and the benefactor of Pepperdine University, lost most of his fortune late in life. Even so, from the valley he found great comfort in all the good he had done. "In the end," he said, "all I had left is what I had given away." What a beautiful reflection from the hardship of valley life.

Thinking, feeling, reflecting, journaling, praying—these are all tools appropriate to the valley. The Psalmist David wrote some of his best poetry in the valley. The list of major leaders who did great writing or formed key ideas in prison is lengthy: Mahatma Gandhi, Dietrich Bonhoeffer, the Apostle Paul, and Nelson Mandela, to name but a few. Chuck Colson's founding and effective leadership of Prison Fellowship Ministry demonstrates that not only can you develop depth and character in the valley, but you will also only be able to help and lead others out of the valley if you have spent some time there yourself.

When It's Time to Move On

You will not want your own condo or a long-term lease on a home in the valley. After you have touched bottom and learned its lessons, you will want to begin your ascent back up from the valley floor. Psychological tests indicate that some people are wired in such a way that they go in and out of the valley of stress fairly easily. Others will not enter the valley as often, but once they do, it takes considerable time and effort to get out. Of course, in the deepest valleys of life, the walls will always be steep and the way out difficult.

One early step is to reengage or reconnect. The valley is such a lonely place that we will begin to feel disconnected from people and even from our own routine and work. Parker Palmer has become a widely consulted resource in higher education and beyond for his work on the spiritual side of life and work. He speaks of the "pain of disconnection," noting that everywhere he goes, he finds faculty who are disconnected from their colleagues, their students, and even their own hearts. David remembers that following the death of his father, for example, it was difficult to see people at first, to reconnect with them. He felt that they were still living life as usual on the plains while he was down in a deep valley. So it is important to reach out, to reestablish connections with family and friends, if only briefly at first. Resuming activities and routines, such as exercise and work, are important first steps out of the bottom of the valley.

It also seems helpful to begin taking positive and proactive steps back toward our work and previous activities. Psychologist William Glasser notes that it is easier to act your way into a better way of feeling than to feel your way into a better way of acting. Although some people may need longer-term therapy to escape the valley, more current psychological thinking encourages shorter-term counseling, with an emphasis on action and not just feeling. Even though we may feel like we have an anchor tied to our leg that is holding us down, we may need to cast that anchor toward higher ground and empower action, first, and let our feelings follow.

Developing a sense of optimism and determination is important in leaving the valley behind. When Beverly Sills took over the New York City Opera in 1979, all the financial indicators were low, and she was putting out fires everywhere. On the opening night of her first opera, the director gave her a plant that died within a week. This really disturbed Sills, so she clipped off one healthy leaf and tossed the rest. She and others cared for the leaf with regularity and determination, and she placed a newspaper headline below the pot: "'I won't be defeated'—Beverly Sills' indomitable spirit is infusing new life into the New York City Opera." The leaf grew into a plant that became a symbol of optimism and determination for the entire crew. Visualizing life outside the valley and developing a will to get there is a key strategy for leaving the valley.

Leadership in the Valley

All that we have said so far reminds us that leaders must themselves know the valley and how to deal with it. But the time will come when they must lead people, and even entire organizations, through the valley experience. Some leaders will inherit difficult circumstances and lead almost constantly through valleys. Nearly all leaders will have to do so at some point in their careers. These tools seem especially important for leaders whose people must traverse the valley.

Cultivate insight and awareness. It is important to understand when your people and your organization are in the valley. Both fear and cynicism are sure to result when people know the company is in the valley but the executives are continuing business as usual. As a seasoned Silicon Valley venture capitalist observed, business leaders are too slow to recognize the valley; they keep thinking that a big turnaround in revenues is just around the corner. It is far better, he says, to admit when things are down and act accordingly. Watch your organization over time, and when the cycle is down, face that honestly. Shepherds recognize and name the valley while others wring their hands hoping it's not true.

Be candid. David and his family were on an airplane over the Atlantic when the plane began making a strange sound. Soon they noticed the flight attendants gathering in the rear. It was clear to them that something fairly serious was wrong, but there was no announcement for some time. Finally, the pilot acknowledged that one of the three engines had gone out and they would have to land in Chicago instead of going as far as Dallas. The failure to share the problem earlier made people more fearful than was necessary. It is generally better for leaders to admit problems rather than to ignore them or appear to hide them. It is well known that the business cycle includes downs as well as ups, and a good shepherd will honestly point out where the organization is rather than try to mask it or ignore it.

Engage people. The Psalmist David says he fears no evil because his leader is with him. In times of crisis or difficulty, it is especially important for leaders to be visible and with people. David Davenport learned in campus crises to let others manage things in the emergency center while he spent his time out with students, the media, and others. He had learned that his presence in the valley was often more important than his decision making.

Find a way to share optimism and hope. Winston Churchill, who led England through the dark valleys of World War II, was a master at this. "All will come right" was one of his favorite phrases. "When you get to the end of your luck," he wrote in the 1930s, "there is a comfortable feeling that you have got to the bottom." His leadership was honest and realistic on one hand, but hopeful and optimistic on the other. Some preparation can be done in advance by helping folks understand that valleys are part of the natural rhythm of life and organizations.

Roll up your sleeves and model a proactive approach. Sometimes shepherds literally put a lamb on their shoulders and carry it up out of the valley. When Lee Iacocca took over Chrysler, it was headed for bankruptcy. He and his fellow leaders took cuts in pay, sought concessions from unions and banks, and borrowed money from the federal government. They worked like there was no tomorrow and soon had Chrysler turned around and making a profit. Sometimes you can work yourself out of the valley, and the sheer engagement in activity can be good for everyone.

Strength from the Valley

President Lyndon Johnson, who was known for his colorful language and stories, said that sometimes as president, he felt like a jackass in a hailstorm: there's nothing to do but to stand there and take it. Leadership can be like that. There will be times when you are personally in a valley but your organization is doing well and needs you. Then there are times you when you are up and the organization is down. And of course there will come a day when it seems like everyone is in the valley.

The leader knows that important growth can occur in the valley. With good leadership, people and organizations should emerge from the valley stronger than when they entered. We see that in America today, following the dark valley of September 11, 2001. Many at the World Trade Center described the sense of literal darkness they felt following the collapse of those twin towers. But from that dark valley grew a spirit of collaboration and patriotism that has, without question, made New York City and America stronger. For both the sheep and the shepherd, the valley need not be a place to fear. Indeed, learning to lead through the valley is one of the highest-order skills of shepherd leadership.

Shepherd Thinking

🖝 What have been some of your valley experiences, both personal and professional?

🖝 When you have experienced valleys, what did you learn from them?

🖝 What kinds of valleys is your organization likely to experience?

Shepherd Doing

🖝 Do a little valley planning with your team. Openly discuss what valleys the organization has experienced or is likely to experience and how you might deal with them and even grow through them.

☛ List what you see as the three most likely valleys you or your organization will face over the next year. Go ahead and allow yourself to think of the worst-case scenario and think through how you would deal with that. If you can handle the worst-case valley in your mind now, you should be able to handle it in reality if and when it comes.

☛ Ask people you work with how they are doing this week. Then wait and really listen to their response. If they are struggling in or near a valley, let them speak a few minutes about that. Allowing someone in a valley to connect with you about it can be an important step on that person's way out.

☛ Taking pen in hand, write out "Un-Psalm 23" from the start of this chapter. As you write, make an effort to empathize with the life of someone in the valley. Such empathy develops your capacity to "be with" your followers.

Chapter Six

Shepherds Come Alongside

I will fear no evil; for Thou art with me.

In the fall of 1996, during David's tenure as president of Pepperdine University in Malibu, California, wildfires threatened the campus. The fires moved quickly, and by dusk, the campus was almost completely surrounded. As a result, all students were urged to stay on campus for two reasons. First, leaving campus by car posed a much greater risk to life and limb than simply sitting in the safety of the well-protected field house. Second, the firefighters needed the already limited Malibu roads to stay clear of traffic so that they could move about as quickly as possible. This proved to be a controversial decision.

Despite being surrounded by the brushlands of the Santa Monica Mountains, Pepperdine's Malibu campus is surprisingly safe in the event of a wildfire. In fact, local firefighters use the campus as their command post whenever wildfires threaten the Malibu area. Nonetheless, it's easy to perceive the campus as a dangerous place to be when wildfires threaten, and that's precisely what happened. Hoping to put a human face on the wildfire drama, the local media began broadcasting stories that might be headlined "Dim-Witted Administrators Hold Students Hostage While Flames Lick Field House Walls." As the story escalated, parents called in demanding that their children be "let go."

The drama peaked as a CNN reporter put David on live television and asked, "What would you tell parents whose children are in that field house tonight?" David responded with two reasonable statements and one completely unexpected statement. He quickly pointed out that the field house was the safest place on campus and also that the firefighters were using it for their headquarters. Then David turned away from his persuasion-oriented legal training and made a simple observation: "Well, my own kids are in there, and if it were not safe, they would not have to be there." After that answer, the media went away and the phone calls stopped.

The Shepherding Paradox

As David demonstrated in the preceding story, shepherding is not an activity that can be done remotely. The shepherd must be present. In our technologically sophisticated age, it's tempting for leaders to trade the classic idea of MBWA ("management by walking around") for MBTA ("managing by typing around"). Unfortunately, cell phones and e-mails are no substitute for "being with." Even walking around is a bit fast paced for the more sedentary "being with" of the shepherd. This brings into sharp focus another paradox of shepherd leadership: there are times when you are up front and times when you are alongside. Even while king of Israel, the Psalmist David found courage when he knew his shepherd was alongside: "I will fear no evil, for thou art with me." Like David, a shepherd leader is both visible leader and vulnerable follower, and often both on the same day.

Part of the shepherding paradox is the need to shift back and forth from leading the macro, big-picture level to the micro, individual-human-being level. Perhaps there was a time when the senior managers handled the big issues and the middle and lower level managers took care of individual needs and problems. But shepherd leaders must both lead the flock and, from time to time, come alongside individual sheep. President George W. Bush and New York City Mayor Rudolph Giuliani were excellent examples of this in the aftermath of the September 11 terrorist attacks. They led the overall disaster and strategic response, but they were also out among their flocks, attending memorial services and comforting families. As head of the American Red Cross, Elizabeth Dole over-saw a staff of nearly thirty-two thousand and a budget of $2 billion but found it important to be out in the field where the relief work was done. That's what shepherd leaders do.

To shepherd effectively, one must know when to lead, when to follow, and when to get out of the way! A shepherd may relinquish the right to lead in certain situations because someone else is better qualified in that area or has more time. Leaders may also follow be-cause they know that another individual's development or that of the team is better served by stepping back from direct leadership and pushing others forward. Part of the paradox is that the people need to know the leader is also there to support them. "What can I do for you? How can I make your work more effective?" These are questions shepherd leaders should constantly be asking their people.

Thinking and Leading Paradoxically

Shepherd leaders need to be both-and, not either-or, thinkers. In today's fluid management environment, and with the complexity of organizations and their problems, the best leaders will be able to embrace the various elements of a paradox or dilemma and find the best balance for the organization. In their classic book *Built to Last*, Jim Collins and Jerry Porras compared the best companies in sev-eral fields with those that were second-best. One of the important distinctions was that the also-ran companies would settle too easily for one side or another of an issue, while the best companies en-gaged in both-and thinking. Am I a macro leader or a micro one? The answer is both. Are we trying to make a profit or act ethically? Both. Are we focusing on our customers or our own people? Both. Am I a leader or a follower? Both.

As with the Psalmist David, the ability to shift back and forth in these various roles and points of view turns out to be one of the fundamental skills of shepherd leaders. In that sense, modern orga-nizations are more like basketball or soccer than football. In foot-ball, players have assigned roles, and only certain people handle the ball or score. But basketball and soccer, reflective of modern organizations, are more fluid, and any player can score. One of the key attributes of technology and the information economy is its incredible speed. Customer needs and products develop so rapidly that business plans are always changing. The key to speed and appropriateness in that environment is not just how fast you can run but how quickly you can change gears.

Shepherd leaders, then, are flexible and able to make transitions well. They can think along more than one track and readily embrace a both-and kind of thinking. More than that, they know they must change roles for the good of the organization and its people, and they are able to shift gears rapidly and smoothly. One key to shepherd leadership is being alongside to notice the changing needs of your followers. As is often said, executives may be *given* subordinates, but they must *earn* followers. By embracing such paradoxes of shepherd leadership, you are constantly earning the right to be followed.

Patient Attention During the Normal Times

Wildfires and other crisis situations are not the only times when a shepherd leader should come alongside his or her followers. A good shepherd is with the flock during the other 99 percent of normal life. Shepherding is not a cruise control situation; attendance and attention are fundamental. The absentee shepherd will quickly find the flock dwindling, if not entirely gone. In the pasture, the shepherd is present to watch the individual sheep for signs of illness. If a sheep is eating well and still not gaining weight, there's a good chance that it is hosting a parasite. If a shepherd fails to notice a slight limp, a sheep can go lame and have to be slaughtered.

The attentive shepherd leader knows the signs of trouble among his followers, and he takes the initiative. More often than not, the shepherd can provide gentle, genuine assistance. Something about human pride keeps us from asking for help even when help is close at hand. The shepherd leader acts perceptively to solve problems by, say, removing irritants, providing resources, or reassigning work.

In today's complex organizations with thousands of employees, it's impossible for a leader to know and care for every single follower. This is clearly a place where the shepherding analogy breaks down if taken too literally. However, the shepherd leader can and must pay attention to their immediate followers. Signs of trouble are as varied as people. An otherwise gregarious follower might suddenly start hiding in his office behind a closed door. For others, a rapid weight gain might suggest that trouble's brewing. Another sign of trouble might be anger and defensiveness from a follower who is usually calm and open. A follower feeling overwhelmed might also procrastinate on assigned projects and start missing deadlines.

A unexpected benefit of coming alongside your followers is that you begin to notice beauty where you might not have seen it before. In a rare case of video encouraging deeper contemplation, art historian Sister Wendy Beckett says that she often experiences beauty when she's filming one of her television appearances. As the crew is setting up for the next shot, Sister Wendy often finds herself parked in front of a piece of art to which she's never given a second glance. More often than not, she begins to warm to the piece as it opens itself up to her. She contends that beauty can be found in almost any work of art if the viewer is patient enough to be with the piece for a while. It may never make your list of personal favorites, but you can admit that it does reflect beauty.

Coming alongside is more than being in the same room or even at the same retreat, so beware of the temptation to fake being with your followers. Working parents often find themselves faking being with their children by talking on the phone while, say, playing a board game with their kids. The parent may think he or she is being clever, but the children realize that even though the parent is in the same room, his or her attention is not on interacting with the children but rather on the business at the other end of the line.

Thus when the shepherd leader is with the follower, he or she is really *with* the follower. Some leaders believe that getting out of the office and walking around a bit signals that you're with your followers. However, it's easy to find yourself speed-walking around the office without ever making eye contact or hall conversation. One highly innovative company intentionally designs its office space to maximize the number of interactions between people in the hallway. They've found that the more people bump into each other in the corridors, the more positive, innovative work gets done. Coming alongside the followers like this can give shepherd leaders a vision of beauty and compassion for their followers. And such a vision fuels our courage when we need to protect our followers.

Courageous Action in Times of Terror

There are some things that servants have never done well, and shepherding is one of them. In the Psalmist David's household, it wasn't the servant who tended the flock but rather a member of the family. Everyone in the ancient Middle East knew that a servant would abandon the sheep and run away when he saw a predator coming. The servant cared more for himself than for the sheep because he was more like a hired hand than a family member. As a family member, the shepherd would stand and fight when the predator came, as he knew that the well-being of the family hinged on his courage.

The Psalmist David spoke of the protective role of the shepherd. Prior to his confrontation with the giant Goliath, the young David is recorded in the Old Testament as telling his king that he has been keeping his father's sheep. "When a lion or bear came and carried off a sheep from the flock, I went after it, struck it and rescued the sheep from its mouth. When it turned on me, I seized it by its hair, struck it and killed it." When danger threatened David's flock, he did not run, nor did he seek permission. Rather, he struck the enemy who endangered his flock. David made a great king because he had learned to be a great shepherd first.

Shepherds bring a sense of vigilance, guidance, and disciplining to the leadership role that's not easily captured by the image of the servant leader. Did you know that you acknowledge the vigilance of the shepherds each holiday season when you sing such well-known Christmas carols as "It Came upon a Midnight Clear," "Angels We Have Heard on High," and, more obviously, "While Shepherds Watched"? Apparently, the announcement of the birth of Jesus came during the dark of the night. With whom could the angels share the glad tidings? The city officials? The merchants? The household servants? No. When everyone else was asleep, the shepherds were keeping a vigilant watch over their flocks in the fields.

Winston Churchill once stated, "Courage is the first of human qualities because it is the quality which guarantees all others." By this he suggests that honesty, conscientiousness, industriousness, and other virtues that keep an organization running would be meaningless if no one courageous enough were around to ensure that virtuous people get the rewards they deserve. Shepherds are called to be courageous. As such, the shepherd leader is much like Gary Cooper in *High Noon*, who faces down a band of evil outlaws by himself as the other men in town make off with a variety of excuses.

The Psalmist David used the word *evil* in this psalm, and shepherd leaders today still use it with no illusions as to the negative impact it will have on their popularity ratings. Thus the shepherd leader must have the courage to judge. Evil runs roughshod over the innocent when leaders stand on the sidelines trying not to judge the actions of others. To label something as "evil" is to make a moral judgment against it. It's an acknowledgment that it's dangerous for the survival of the organization and the well-being of the followers. Shepherd leaders must use such moral language to unveil genuine threats to a firm and alert their followers to the danger. Piracy, confidence games, technology hacking, embezzlement, and the like cannot just be labeled as "different" but must be labeled as "wrong" and dealt with courageously.

The shepherd leader must also have the courage to act. The courage to act is less about the physical courage of attacking a bear and more about mental courage. Mental courage requires lining up your values and priorities in advance of a threatening situation and not compromising according to the vicissitudes of a situation. Political philosopher Edmund Burke noted that "the only thing necessary for evil to triumph is for good people to do nothing." Shortly before a group of business travelers rushed the cockpit to stop the terrorists who had seized control of United Air Lines flight 93, Todd Beamer led them in a recitation of the Psalm 23. Beamer, Thomas Burnett, and others would succeed in stopping the terrorists from crashing the plane in its intended target. We suspect that Psalm 23 was more than a source of religious consolation for these heroes. Rather, we believe that the psalm was a source of courage, strength, and power.

David: Both Leader and Follower

One reason Psalm 23 works for both leaders and followers is that its author, David, played both roles. The idea of viewing life in a shepherding context did not occur to David at random or from reading a book. Rather, he spent countless hours tending the family flock. Shepherding affords plenty of time for thought and reflection, and we can readily envision David, out under the starry sky at night, thinking about how life—in his case, life with God, specifically—is very much like shepherding. Even as David was leading his own flock, he was coming to understand how his leader, God, shepherded him.

Then one day God's prophet, Samuel, was told to look in the household of Jesse, David's father, for a king for Israel. One by one, Jesse's sons were brought before Samuel, and each time the prophet said no, this is not the future king. Finally, after each of these strapping sons had been rejected, Samuel asked, are there no more? Jesse answered that he had yet one more son, his youngest, David, but he was out tending sheep. The implication was that David, the runt of the family, was not kingly material. Samuel asked them to bring the young shepherd in, and when he met David, he said, this is Israel's future king, for God looks not at the outward appearance but into the heart.

Like all great leaders, David led with his strength. If you are a coach, you tend to lead like one, even in nonathletic settings. If you are a teacher, your natural leadership style is that of a teacher and mentor. David was a shepherd, so even as a king, he exercised what we have come to call shepherd leadership. But there were also times he was led, and he wrote his best-known poem, Psalm 23, from his perspective as a sheep being shepherded. One of the powerful paradoxes of this great poem is that its author knew shepherd leadership from both sides, as a shepherd and as a sheep.

Shepherd Thinking

- Are there situations in life in which you are a leader and others in which you follow? Which do you prefer? Which are you better at? How well do you shift from one to the other?
- Ask yourself: What's my basis of authority? Do people follow me because I'm alongside or because they are afraid of what I can do to them?
- What are the most serious dangers facing your company?

Shepherd Doing

- Get to know your followers better by knowing their signs of trouble. Write down the signs of trouble for each of your immediate followers. Then review the list with them and inquire about its accuracy.
- Make a list of positive characteristics for each of your immediate followers. Pay attention and try to capture what's unique and wonderful about each of them. Keep this list to yourself, and return to it often to cultivate a vision of beauty for each of your followers.
- Prepare a basic plan for dealing with the serious dangers that threaten your company.

✒ Like the Psalmist David, write something from the point of view of one of your followers. Work to step inside their skin and see life under your leadership from their perspective.

Chapter Seven

Shepherds Use the Right Tools

Thy rod and thy staff, they comfort me.

Perhaps you saw the announcement:

Major Technological Breakthrough!

Announcing the new Built-in Orderly Organized Knowledge device known as the BOOK.

The BOOK is a revolutionary breakthrough in technology: No wires, no electric circuits, no batteries, nothing to be connected or switched on. It's so easy to use even a child can operate it. Just lift its cover!

Compact and portable, it can be used anywhere—even sitting in an armchair by the fire—yet it is powerful enough to hold as much information as a CD-ROM! Here's how it works: . . . Each BOOK is constructed of sequentially numbered sheets of (recyclable) paper, each capable of holding thousands of bits of information. These pages are locked together with a custom-fit device called a binder that keeps the sheets in their correct sequence. . . .

Portable, durable, and affordable, the BOOK is being hailed as the entertainment wave of the future. The BOOK's appeal seems so certain that thousands of content creators have committed to the platform. Look for a flood of new titles soon.

To the young generation of the twenty-first century, tools like rods and staffs, or even books, must seem quaintly old-fashioned. Two of David's children were stumped on research questions, since the answers were not immediately discoverable on-line, until he introduced them to an old standby: the almanac. They were amazed that a book could reveal in mere moments data that had eluded them through technology. Thanks to scientific calculators, few students have even heard of a slide rule. And who uses calendars or phone books when you have personal data assistants (PDAs) and on-line directories? Equipping kids for school today is a very different experience from going to the dime store for a Big Chief tablet and some Elmer's glue.

The Low-Tech Tools of Shepherding

By contrast, even today, shepherding is a low-tech occupation, as it certainly was in ancient Israel. There is the more modern, higher-tech field of sheep ranching and production, but it has not totally supplanted old-fashioned shepherding. In modern sheep ranching, like cattle production, the emphasis is on aggressive feeding and supplements so that the animals mature more rapidly and get to market as quickly as possible. In recent years, many consumers have begun expressing a preference for meat from animals that are raised in more natural ways and not by the accelerated means of production. Who knows, shepherds may be on the ascendancy in this high-tech world.

The Psalmist describes two tools that were part of every shepherd's equipment, the rod and the staff, as sources of comfort. The shepherd's rod was a wooden club or stick that served several purposes. Its primary use was to discipline the sheep, providing the shepherd with a tool to move the animals here or there or block their progress in an undesired direction. The rod might also be used to inspect the sheep in a close and intimate way. As the sheep left the gate, the rod would stop them and then be used to open their fleece for examination. Finally, and most dramatically, the shepherd would use the rod to ward off predators by throwing it with practiced speed and accuracy.

Likewise, the shepherd's staff was a multipurpose tool. Its unique crook allowed the shepherd to catch sheep and move them about, perhaps pulling an animal out of water or away from danger. In the larger flock, a lamb could easily become separated from its mother, and the staff would allow the shepherd to draw the little one back where it belonged. The staff was even a support for the shepherd, who might lean on it in the fields, and a guide for the sheep. Today a rifle often replaces the rod, but the staff is still very much in use and is widely recognized as the hallmark of the shepherd.

A tool kit should reflect the tasks of the workman. On the old *What's My Line?* TV show, where panelists asked yes-or-no questions to figure out a guest's occupation, showing the tools of the worker would in many cases have been a dead giveaway. A rolling pin suggests flattening and stretching dough, the task of a baker. The rod and staff, whose purposes are guiding, disciplining, and protecting sheep, tell us those are the primary tasks of the shepherd.

The Shepherd Leader's Tool Kit

What, then, are the tools of the modern shepherd leader? The question is not an easy one, since shepherd leaders might work in a number of fields, with a variety of constituencies, in pursuit of vastly different goals and objectives. Amid so many variables, are there common tools of shepherd leaders? If so, how might they be identified?

Before attempting to answer those important questions, it is only fair to note that to some degree, the tools of any leader begin with his or her individual strengths. John Sculley, who came to Apple from Pepsi, had a very different skill set than computer guru Steve Jobs. Yet each of these leaders has been successful by drawing on his own skills and abilities. It is almost always a mistake to try to emulate someone else's leadership style or skills. Instead, you must find your own skills and tools and work from those strengths as consistently as possible. Even in midcareer, some of the psychological tests that reveal your strengths and style can be very worthwhile investments in identifying your best tools.

Another factor is that an organization's needs at particular points in its history will vary, suggesting that different tools may be needed from time to time. It is almost axiomatic in start-ups and technology companies, for example, that the skill set of the entre-preneur who launches a company is not what will be needed to grow and professionalize the firm. Sometimes leaders can adapt and develop new tools; more often they either shape the management team to cover those needs or give way to a new leader with the tools needed by the corporation at that time. Frequently, an organization will want a leader with different skills than his predecessor. Before David led Pepperdine University, a quiet, grandfatherly scholar, Howard White, had succeeded a dynamic young president, Bill Banowsky. Each was effective in his own way and was what the institution needed at the time.

Acknowledging, then, that the tools of a shepherd leader will vary according to the needs of the organization and the skills of the individual manager, are there any standard tools that shepherd lead-ers should possess? Are there modern-day equivalents of the rod and staff that were of comfort to the Psalmist David? To answer that question, we need first to remember the purpose of those ancient tools: to guide, discipline, and protect the sheep. If you could choose only two tools for that purpose today, what would you se-lect? We know our choices. Let us make the case that no shepherd leader today should be without a compass and a frame.

The Compass

One odd aspect of living on the California coast is that you never quite know which direction is north. You would think that it would be an easy calculation. If the ocean is on your left and the moun-tains or valley on your right, you are facing north, correct? The truth is, it's not that simple. In fact, the coastline of California does not run directly north and south; it juts and curves, with confusing bays and inlets and craggy points. Living in Malibu, which is partly on Santa Monica Bay and partly on the Pacific Ocean, is especially confusing. If you're looking at the ocean, which according to the California map in your head should be west, you're actually facing south.

In many ways, this is comparable to trying to find your direction in organizational life today. Data and information flow so rapidly, and products and services must respond so quickly, that the landscape is in a constant state of turmoil and change. They say that one reason lightning never strikes the same place twice is that the same place isn't there anymore, and they're right. Businesses that used to make five-year plans are now fortunate if a one-year business plan will remain relevant. Corporate executives have coined a new term for seeing out ahead in this environment: visibility. We cannot make solid forecasts, they will say, because there is no visibility at the present time. How would you like to be flying on a plane where the pilot admits there is basically no visibility?

If you are fortunate to attend a conference led by Stephen Covey, he may ask you to close your eyes and point north. When you open your eyes and look around, there will be fingers pointing in literally every conceivable direction. He sometimes asks his audience to close their eyes again, admitting that it was a little unfair since many of the participants are not from the local area and might be confused. Covey will suggest that this time only those who are really sure about the direction point their fingers north. Again, CEOs and senior leaders are pointing everywhere. He goes on to talk about the importance of knowing where "true north" is in any organization and leadership's role in making that plain.

All the metaphors of organizational life today suggest that the compass, an ancient and simple instrument, is one of the most valuable tools a leader can have in the tool kit. People describe the landscape today as one of chaos, as in a blinding snowstorm or permanent white-water rapids. In that kind of setting, where people have to make rapid-fire decisions among a bewildering array of choices, one of the greatest needs is a clear statement of the values and overall direction of the organization from the leadership. Like the rod and staff, the compass provides the sort of guidance, and even protection from competitors and enemies, that will keep things on track.

In the wonderful movie *Mr. Holland's Opus*, Richard Dreyfus plays a composer who turned to teaching high school music, intending to stay just a few years but instead spending his entire life there. Early in his career as a teacher, Mr. Holland had some difficulty reaching students. In a memorable conversation with the school principal, she advised him that a teacher has two jobs: "Fill young minds with knowledge, yes, but more important, give those minds a compass so that that knowledge doesn't go to waste."

In many ways, a compass, which provides a sense of overall direction, is more valuable today than the shepherd's rod or even a map. The rod is a tool for micromanagers, telling individual sheep which path to take. It will never empower the follower and will always limit the scope and impact of the leader. The map is slightly better, providing a sense of the larger journey, but it still represents a form of micromanagement—first you travel from A to B, then from B to C. What people really need is the compass, the sense of overall direction, so that wherever they are, they can move in the right way.

Educational leaders point north when they remind their teachers and staff to keep students first in mind and to stand at all times for integrity and excellence. And then they must model that by putting students first in their own administrative decisions, where the rubber meets the road. Research has shown that college students, for example, often learn as much from the implicit or hidden curriculum—the way teachers talk and act and the way the college is run—as they do from the formal curriculum. Likewise, business and other leaders must tirelessly proclaim and practice the fundamental values of their organizations so that in quick decisions or in difficult times, followers will know where true north really is.

The Frame

The second tool is more difficult to name. Some people might picture it as a playing field. Others have described it as a box or container. Here we choose to call it a frame. The common thread is that shepherd leaders must build some kind of context in which the primary stakeholders make decisions and move organizations forward. It is up to the leader to lay out the playing field, to build the container, to establish the framework where the followers can do their work. Then let them go at it!

Here, of course, the shepherd-and-sheep analogy begins to reach some of its limitations. Shepherds do build fields or pastures for sheep, defining them with a fence or, today, some good dogs. But sheep do not really engage in much independent thought or action, and the purpose of building a field is not really to empower the sheep to make good decisions. That is, however, the purpose of the shepherd leader's frame: to establish some boundaries in which the real stakeholders of decisions, those whose life and work will be most affected by them, will step up and take ownership. That is the empowering work of today's shepherd leaders.

As Ronald Heifetz, in his classic book *Leadership Without Easy Answers*, explains, in an earlier day, we often turned to leaders because they had greater expertise than we do. They had more knowledge, or experience, or training in a particular field, which is why they were selected as leaders. A classic example is the medical field, where we submit to the leadership and diagnosis of doctors because we understand that they have greater expertise than we do. Today, however, there is simply too much to know in many organizations and in the rapidly changing environment. Leaders cannot possibly know more than their followers about everything. So in most organizations, we must look to leaders for a different reason, and leaders must do a different kind of work.

The primary work of leadership today is to build the context or frame in which organizations make decisions and move forward. It is easier to see the idea initially by looking at how we raise children.

As parents of young children, we build a protective wall around them and direct or take care of their every move. But as they become older, we must be flexible and stretch the boundaries a bit, allowing them some independent thought and action. By the time they are teenagers, we are desperately trying to hold that frame in place, giving where we can, holding where we must, as they become empowered as young adults. If we do not, as parents, build ever-larger frames, our children's growth will be stunted, or they will simply jump the fence.

The great temptation on the part of leaders—and followers—is to rely on leaders to make all the important decision and even some of the unimportant ones. But there are many problems with this model, in which followers are essentially framing decisions for leaders, rather than vice versa. For one thing, the followers will never grow and develop in appropriate ways. Their own decision-making muscles will atrophy. In addition, leaders cannot be in enough different places at the right time for this model to work in the fast-track world in which we live. Yet another problem is that stakeholders in the decision will develop resentments for decisions that leaders are making.

A classic example of this erroneous approach is what in basketball is sometimes called the "matador defense." Apparently coined in the days of Bill Russell and the great Boston Celtics championship teams, the matador defense describes a situation in which it became tempting for the guards, or those playing defense nearest the ball, to let their man through because they knew they had the greatest defensive center in basketball back by the basket to stop things. At times it almost appeared that the little guys would wave the bull, matador style, through to the big fella. Well, lo and behold, the big fella could not stop every drive, and whenever he dropped off his defensive assignment to pick up someone else's, things began to break down.

How often do we see the matador defense in organizational life today? People want to wave decisions through to the big leaders, hoping to defer responsibility and hard work. Shepherd leaders, however, do not allow this to happen. They are actively building a frame in which stakeholders—those who must live with the decisions that are made—make their own decisions. Generally, the people closest to the action will have the most information to bring to the decision. And those who must live with the decision over the long term are apt to see the right direction or make a course correction if they turn out to be wrong. At General Electric, Jack Welch insisted that other corporate officers, and not the CEO, make all business decisions involving $25 million or less. He might advise them, but he did not allow the decisions to be passed through to him.

Corporate giants David Packard and William Hewlett exemplified building the frame and letting people work creatively within it. They realized that as an engineering company, they depended on the creativity of their people. So they spent most of their time developing what came to be known as the "H-P way." In fact, when Packard was once asked what product decisions were most important in Hewlett-Packard's success, his response was not about products but about building the organization frame, with engineering teams, profit sharing, financial discipline, and the like. And now H-P CEO Carly Fiorina faces the challenge of translating the H-P way to a larger organization following the merger with Compaq and its rather different corporate culture.

What does building the frame look like? Sometimes it looks like doing nothing. One otherwise impressive leader sometimes seemed lazy or inattentive until we learned that he was quietly shepherding all the while. He would allow things to fall on the ground and make a mess rather than dive at the last minute to catch them. It was his way of forcing others to step up. Often building the frame is coming alongside folks and talking with them about the challenges they face and how they are approaching those challenges. Guiding them to see the necessary data and information and helping them frame the precise question to be answered in a decision can be crucial. At its very best, shepherd leadership will be more about helping people understand the questions than giving out a lot of answers. Building the frames and waiting for people to step up to their responsibilities requires the patience, faith, and wisdom of a great shepherd leader.

Shepherd Thinking

🖝 Looking at your own gifts and abilities, what are the two or three best tools you have?

🖝 Looking at the development of the organization you lead— family, work, church—what tools are most needed now?

🖝 What is "north" for your organization? What are its core values and directions?

Shepherd Doing

🖝 Try to spot the "matador defense" in your daily work, and turn the responsibility back to the individuals who should shoulder it.

🖝 As you go through your day or week, list the decisions that need to be made. Then note who the primary stakeholders are for each decision. Are they making the key decisions?

🖝 Count how many times in a day or week you mention the core values and directions of your organization. Try to double it. (That will still not be enough!)

🖝 Create a list of terminable offenses for your company, and communicate your list to your followers. This helps set a frame for judging appropriate behavior.

Chapter Eight

Shepherds Transform Conflict

Thou preparest a table before me in the presence
of mine enemies.

Jack Willome's customers were suing him. At the time, Willome
was president of Rayco, a very successful home builder in San
Antonio, Texas. For a variety of reasons, an attorney rallied a number of homeowners to join a lawsuit against Rayco that could very
well destroy the company. After much personal prayer and wise
counsel from friends, Willome made the unexpected decision to sit
through forty-five days of depositions as one homeowner after
another filed through to describe Willome and his company in the
worst possible terms.

Willome found the process very painful but came to realize that
these homeowners had genuine needs and concerns about his company or else they wouldn't be in court. In an interview some years
later, he remarked, "I believe that where the compassion of Christ
comes in is to be able to see the innocence of people who are
attacking you." His ability to see the innocence in his adversary's
viewpoint allowed him to grasp knowledge of truths and perceive
a fundamental fairness that had eluded him up to that point. As a
result, Willome managed to settle the case before going to trial.
Willome also left the experience with a deeper knowledge of the
needs and concerns of first-time home buyers that allowed him to
revitalize Rayco in the late 1980s. By the time he sold the company
in 1996, Rayco had achieved an astounding 40 percent share of the
market for new home closings in San Antonio.

Willome's story reminds us that life is far from a steady stream of green pastures and quiet waters. Psalm 23 takes yet another dark turn at this point. The verse begins with the shepherd taking care of needs by "preparing a table" for the sheep. Rather than being a quiet corner table, this table is "in the presence of mine enemies." It is this final word that provides the theme for this chapter. Life in the field and in the marketplace is full of enemies—and this means conflict.

Trouble in the Fields

Sheep are relatively peaceful creatures, but even they are not without conflict. Chicken coops have the "pecking order," and flocks of sheep have the "butting order." This butting order can have both healthy and unhealthy consequences for the flock, and we'll discuss each. The healthiest manifestation of the butting order is during the mating season, when rams clash with one another for the attention and affection of ewes. This annual conflict ensures that only the strongest and healthiest rams sire the next generation of sheep, thereby maximizing the survival chances of the flock over the long run. Mating contests such as these are as old as creation and have served animals well, as offspring must be strong and healthy to survive in the wild. Should a well-intentioned shepherd establish a zero-tolerance butting policy, he would guarantee the destruction of his flock. It might take a season or two, but his flock will dwindle as disease and weakness start to take their toll.

Just as the shepherd must withhold his hand in the presence of healthy conflict, he must wield his authority when the butting order negatively affects his flock. Butting isn't just limited to the mating season, and shepherds might witness butting during feeding times if a dominant ram decides to drive anyone and everyone away from "his" grass or "his" water. In such situations, the shepherd simply takes the ram by the horns and puts him in a pen all by himself. These rams may be the dominant leaders in the flock, but if they keep otherwise healthy sheep from eating and drinking, the flock will become full of weak sheep, ultimately decreasing its size. The good shepherd sees a bigger picture and knows that both he and the flock are better off in the long run when all sheep have access to basic necessities like food and water.

Shepherds Create a Healthy Space for Conflict

In the same way, shepherd leaders exert their legitimate authority to keep destructive self-promoting behaviors in check. Shepherd leaders understand that conflict is not to be avoided but rather to be transformed into a process that gives life and health to their followers. In preparation for this transformation, the shepherd prepares a space where a healthy kind of disagreement can occur. Just as mating rivalries among sheep are necessary to produce the healthiest flock possible, healthy disagreements are necessary to keep a business on track and out of trouble. Chewing gum entrepreneur William Wrigley captured this idea when he said, "When two people in business *always* agree, one of them is unnecessary." An important first step in fostering healthy conflict is for the shepherd leader to both teach and model to followers that they can disagree without being disagreeable.

Unfortunately, many disagreements can quickly escalate into lawsuits or worse. The shepherd leader knows the patterns of escalation and acts early to ensure that only legitimate disagreements move into court. During David Davenport's presidency at Pepperdine, a benefactor left a major bequest that had the potential to end up in dispute between Pepperdine and another university. Rather than going through the lawyers, David called the president of the other institution and asked him if he was aware of the dispute. He informed David that his attorneys had already briefed him on the situation. David proposed that the two presidents meet alone for breakfast and try to resolve it before turning it over to the lawyers and, most likely, the press. The two of them met and agreed on a fair settlement based on what they believed to be the intent of the donor.

Sometimes the shepherd leader must transform an aggressive first blow into a creative deal-making opportunity. In 1997, Digital Equipment Corporation brought an unexpected patent infringement suit against Intel, alleging that Intel had misappropriated technology from Digital to create the profitable Pentium chip line. The situation began to escalate when leaders from both firms awakened to the possibility that they might be better off going forward as partners rather than adversaries. Should Digital win and alienate Intel, Intel might partner with one of Digital's competitors and drive Digital out of business. Should Intel win, it would most likely do so at great loss to its positive reputation. In the end, leaders from both sides considered both the merits of the case and the merits of a better partnership and decided to go forward with a value-creating partnership instead of a value-destroying lawsuit.

Researchers who study conflict in organizations distinguish between two main types of conflict: interpersonal conflict and intellectual conflict. Interpersonal conflict is almost always dysfunctional, but intellectual conflict can result in a number of positive outcomes if managed properly. Interpersonal conflict happens when people attack one another because they either don't like each other or because each feels threatened by the other. It's characterized by behaviors such as abusive name-calling, intimidation tactics, political retaliation, and escalation. It's never about what's best for the company or about which program, person, or idea has more merit. Rather, it's about destroying the other person. In the extreme, it's about "me winning big" and "you losing everything." Attitudes and behaviors like this set the stage for destructive interpersonal conflict in which everyone involved loses. Like the dominant ram on an unchecked butting spree, interpersonal conflict undermines relationships, creativity, and ultimately morale.

Shepherd leaders can promote more intellectual conflict and less interpersonal conflict by viewing conflict more like a boxing match than a free-for-all slugfest. Unlike a street fight, boxers in a ring follow an established set of rules as they exchange blows, and a referee is present to witness and correct any breech of these rules. Intellectual conflict is very similar. Think of it as a disagreement governed by a set of social rules and a shepherd acting as referee. Labeling someone's idea "racist" is not intellectual conflict but name-calling (and that falls within the realm of interpersonal conflict). Clearly demonstrating how this same person's idea will have adverse impact on minority populations is intellectual conflict. The shepherd's role is to notice name-calling and other destructive interpersonal behaviors and to insist that the person critique the idea on its intellectual merits instead of merely attacking the other person.

Ultimately, the shepherd leader works to create a culture where healthy intellectual conflict can flourish and destructive interpersonal conflict can be held in check. The Supreme Court of the United States seems to have benefited from such leadership in the past. In the fall of 2000, Supreme Court Justice Clarence Thomas took to the airwaves to address the popular conception of a "bitterly divided" Court in the wake of the Court's landmark *Bush v. Gore* ruling. He stated that the Supreme Court might be divided, but it certainly wasn't a bitter division. In fact, he said he found the Court the most civil place he'd ever worked, due mainly to the traditional use of the phrase "I respectfully dissent" in fostering an atmosphere of healthy intellectual conflict among the justices. Justice Thomas stated that the phrase is used to imply many things: I respect your knowledge of the law. I respect the oath you took to uphold the Constitution. I respect your position of authority on this Court. And I disagree. Here are my reasons . . . The habitual use of this and other phrases help create a space where disagreement fuels a more civil workplace rather than undermines morale.

Shepherds Create a Space for Reconciliation

Reconciliation is difficult work. To make matters worse, most of us are more skilled in breaking off relationships than putting them back together. The good news is that reconciliation is a learnable skill, and you get better with practice. Here you'll find the basic steps you need to take in a reconciliation effort.

Set the table. The shepherd in this verse looks more like a dinner host than a leader, and that's precisely how you need to think about it. The Psalmist David understood that a strong leader could set a table where followers and their enemies could gather in hopes of resolving conflict. This was his attitude when he wrote the line "Thou preparest a table before me in the presence of mine enemies." A surprising amount of life's most important moments happen over a meal. Look back over your own life and think about how many of your life's key moments have happened at mealtime. Marriage proposals, pregnancy announcements, promotion decisions, and peacemaking, among other things, will probably come to mind.

When people get lost in a disagreement, the situation can spiral out of control, making it difficult to find a way back to agreement. This is exactly when a third party, like a shepherd leader, can step in and lead the parties out of the wilds of an escalating conflict. Arranging for enemies to sit down at a common table may be the one act that pays the best dividends. If you have trouble getting people to come to the table, fill it with food. Should you need any convincing or inspiration, watch the Academy Award–winning film *Babette's Feast*. In this film, a wise cook fosters reconciliation among a factious group of people by preparing a meal so sumptuous that they cannot help but enjoy themselves in one another's company. *Babette's Feast* illustrates that much depends on dinner, especially when it comes to peacemaking.

Make room for two or more perspectives. Once you're all together, recall the incident, and ask the parties to explain what it looked like from their perspective. Expect to hear a different view from everyone involved. Sure, there will be some overlap, but expect more divergence than convergence. When one party has finished speaking, avoid the temptation to ask, "Do you agree with what so-and-so just said?" for the answer will almost certainly be a resounding no. Rather, ask the other party, "So how do you see it differently?" It will amaze you how different the same incident can look from each side of the table.

Just like setting the table, getting everyone's story out is an underestimated step in reconciliation. A startling amount of conflict is caused by sheer miscommunication and misunderstanding due to our basic human limitations in both perceiving and processing information. Some conflicts will evaporate whenever a forum is established where information can be reviewed and clarified. Also, sitting at a common table is often the first time each party genuinely comes to realize that the other party is truly hurting or truly frustrated. The answer is not to hide the emotional outbursts away in private rooms. Rather, it's having a shepherd present to move things forward as emotions emerge rather than having emotions escalate the situation.

Uncover good intentions and negative impacts. As you listen to the two stories, be sure to probe for both good intentions and negative impacts. As Doug Stone, Bruce Patton, and Sheila Heen point out in their book *Difficult Conversations*, parties in conflict are highly motivated to save face, and letting them say that they had good intentions helps them do this. Unfortunately, our efforts to help can have a negative impact on the other party. The shepherd leader needs to honor good intentions while at the same time pointing out the hurtful impact each party's actions had on the other.

Good intentions help each party feel less suspicious of the other. Uncovering hurtful impacts helps each party realize that it has harmed the other party even though that may never have been the intention. Should it become clear that one party intentionally set out to harm the other party, the shepherd leader is present to witness the information and provide the necessary pressure on the hurtful party to find a way to put things right without having to resort to legal remedies. By this point, the stage is set for the final part of the reconciliation.

Invite an apology and other healing words. Successful reconciliations are not necessarily characterized by brilliant breakthrough solutions and weepy reunions. At a minimum, the shepherd should invite an apology from each side. Some parties might object to this as a complete capitulation and refuse. These people are probably falling victim to the all-or-nothing syndrome, which tells them either they are 100 percent right or 100 percent wrong. Apologies, like enemies, are rarely 100 percent entities. An apology can be as simple as "I am sorry that I misunderstood you" or "I am sorry that my actions caused you such frustration." These apologies are a long way from the 100 percent apology of "I am sorry; I was completely wrong in this situation." Your invitation might only be that of asking each party to apologize for the painful impact it has had on the other party. Often this negative impact is completely unintentional, and the parties both save face through their otherwise good intentions.

A good shepherd can also encourage each party to express goodwill for the future of the relationship. Sometimes each party will express hopes that the relationship can return to better terms in the future. Sometimes one party will express goodwill and the other party only scowls. This is when the shepherd must focus on the rightness of the action rather than just the immediate results. Regardless of negative reactions, the joint opportunity to express goodwill and words of healing has the potential to plant a seed for the future. It's difficult to remain a complete enemy with someone who hoped a better future for you.

The shepherd in Psalm 23 did not shrink in the presence of conflict. Rather, he viewed such conflict as an opportunity to sit down at a common table and work things out. Likewise, the modern shepherd leader is alert to the danger of escalation and seeks to create a space where both reconciliation and healthy conflict can occur. Should unhealthy conflict persist despite your best efforts, take heart! University of Washington researcher John Gottman observed marriages over a period of years and found that on average, over two-thirds of the conflicts in the marriages remain unresolved. So if you've worked to create a space for healthy conflict and for reconciliation only to discover that you can't resolve the conflict, you are not without options. Sometimes a shepherd leader's best option is to manage the conflict by putting as much room as possible between the two adversaries. Space is underrated as a means to controlling the costs of conflict. Just ask the shepherd who locks problem rams in separate pens.

Shepherd Thinking

☞ Who is my enemy, and how do I know this?

☞ Where in my life do I make myself look better than I am and vilify others as worse than they probably are?

☞ Where are the broken or strained relationships in my work life (or even personal life) that are in need of reconciliation?

☞ Where are the broken or strained relationships among my followers that are in need of reconciliation?

Shepherd Doing

☞ Draft a set of rules to guide intelligent conflict among your followers. How should problem-solving meetings work? What behaviors are off-limits? How do you signal that a "personal foul" just occurred?

☞ Take action in the coming weeks to reconcile a broken or strained relationship in your own work life or personal life. Write out a script for yourself in advance, following the steps outlined in this chapter. Focus on the rightness of reconciliation rather than on breakthrough results, as the other party may not respond immediately or may even react negatively. Nevertheless, you will plant an important seed.

☞ Create a table for reconciliation for two of your followers— but not before you've practiced reconciliation in your own life. Avoid the temptation to dramatically reconcile bitter enemies. Rather, find relationships that have been strained or broken by simple misunderstandings or petty grudges.

Chapter Nine

Shepherds Remove Irritants

Thou anointest my head with oil.

The Philadelphia economy was struggling in the 1750s, and no one could comprehend why. Other cities in Colonial America—especially Boston and New York—were growing. It's not that life was wretched in the City of Brotherly Love; it was just vaguely unpleasant, and no one could put his finger on what was wrong. No one, that is, except Benjamin Franklin.

When economies are struggling, big fixes are often tempting. The city leaders in Philadelphia could have tried any number of expensive solutions. They could have built more wharves and warehouses to increase trade. They could have improved the roads leading to the city or hired a full-time militia to increase security. Benjamin Franklin made a small and rather curious recommendation: hire some street sweepers.

Franklin observed a great deal of dust swirling around the streets of the commercial district in Philadelphia. When the dust got bad, two things happened: the local shopkeepers kept their doors closed, and people sought the comfort of home rather than the irritation of the streets. When a few people were paid to keep the streets as dust-free as possible, people returned to the commercial district, and business picked up. "Some may think these trifling matters not worth minding," Franklin would later write in his autobiography. Dust in one person's eyes, admittedly, is an inconvenience. Dust in everyone's eye, he argued, could seriously hamper a city's economic and social vitality. "Human happiness," Franklin continued, "is produced not so much by great pieces of good fortune that seldom happen, as by little advantages that occur every day."

Shepherd leaders are certainly wise to seize the "great pieces of good fortune that seldom happen." However, it's a foolish leader that lets a thousand and one small opportunities for improvement slip away while pinning all hopes on another big event. Why? Because a better life for your followers is more often a product of the "little advantages that occur every day." At times the advantage is gained by adding something beneficial. More often, as in Franklin's case, it's gained by removing something irritating.

A Sheep's Worst Enemy

A defining characteristic of sheep is their herding instinct. They are programmed to stick together, and they do so better than almost any other animal. The good news is that this makes the shepherd's task much easier. The bad news is that it significantly increases the chance for disease. In fact, there's an old saying among shepherds that "a sheep's worst enemy is another sheep." Dysentery, tetanus, foot-and-mouth disease, and even pneumonia can sweep through a flock of sheep if left unchecked. Furthermore, a variety of internal and external parasites can move from sheep to sheep with remarkable rapidity. Nematodes pass between sheep by living in the pasture grass, and they can kill a sheep in a matter of days if unnoticed and untreated.

A real scourge in the fields is the beginning of fly season each summer. The aptly named head fly can literally drive a sheep crazy when it swarms during fly season. The nose fly can be just as bad as it dive-bombs the sheep, attempting to lay eggs in the sheep's soft, moist nasal cavity. At a minimum, a sheep will stop grazing and hide in the protection of the brush when afflicted by flies. At worst, a sheep will ram its head into the ground, a post, or another sheep when swarmed by either of these flies. A horde of flies left unchecked can transform a peaceful, healthy flock into a skittish, ailing herd.

The Psalmist David knew exactly how to deal with such illnesses and irritants in the field. He would anoint, or medicate, his sheep by rubbing ointments on their heads and faces. Hence the phrase "Thou anointest my head with oil." This ointment repelled the flies and allowed the sheep to continue grazing in peace. As the effects of the ointment faded and the flies returned, the shepherd would come around again for another application—witness once again to the need for present and attentive shepherds. Even in modern times, shepherds anoint their sheep with a variety of medications and ointments. The smallest nick while shearing wool can turn nasty if not covered with a smear to keep the flies away.

Removing the Irritants

Ask a real shepherd about the key to successful shepherding, and he'll say, "Shepherding is the easiest job in the world once you get your sheep vaccinated . . . and get the head flies under control . . . and the screw worm . . . and the liver fluke . . . and . . ." Every shepherd knows that the size and health of one's flock is limited when irritants run rampant. When shepherds in the field get rid of the irritants, the size and health of the flock increase dramatically. Graphically, it looks like this:

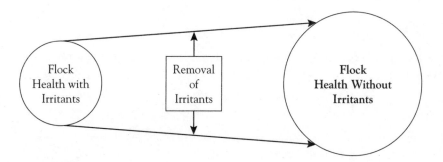

The same principles apply for the shepherd leader. Gordon Binder discovered this when he was CEO of Amgen. Amgen is a biotech firm full of researchers and scientists possessing the most advanced degrees in their field. Binder did not have to motivate his core workers, nor did he have to tell them what to do. He concluded that his job was to listen to his people and remove the irritants and obstacles that they believed were blocking their path. In the absence of obstacles and irritants, his followers did what they were trained to do, and the business flourished.

In the field, the sheep rarely run to the shepherd when there's trouble. Rather, it's more often the shepherd who must seek out the sheep and check for problems. Imagine the two vastly different perspectives in the field between the shepherd and the sheep. From the shepherd's perspective, the irritation is a group of flies easily driven away with some ointment. From the perspective of the sheep, however, it is a pestilence that they have no power to stop. That's why one of the hallmarks of shepherd leadership is the ability to view one's followers with a deep sense of compassion. Rather than despising one's "weak-minded" followers for struggling with what you see as an insect-sized problem, one is moved by compassion to serve the followers on their terms when necessary. When it comes to being a shepherd leader, it might be good advice to "sweat the small stuff."

So what might be some common irritants afflicting your followers? If you polled your followers, chances are that the word *uncertainty* would appear somewhere on the short list. Of course, some followers will find uncertainty invigorating, seeing opportunity within all the chaos. Many, however, will find uncertainty frightening and will await instruction rather than take a risk. This is when the shepherd leader comes alongside to clarify roles, directions, expectations, and the like. Others might cry "bureaucracy," and the shepherd moves in to remove outdated control systems and replace them with more agile service models.

Another common affliction might be low self-efficacy. The notion of self-efficacy was popularized by motivation theorist Albert Bandura. Put simply, Bandura contends that individuals with low

self-efficacy do not believe they have the ability to overcome what-
ever challenge they face. This challenge can be as simple as logging
on to a networked computer or as daunting as mounting a legal
battle against a formidable foe. The good news is that a shepherd
leader can come alongside the follower and build self-efficacy a variety of ways.

Bandura's research demonstrates that one route to higher self-
efficacy is simply talking with the follower. This conversation can
be either some words of encouragement and confidence, or it can be
a story about how a person similar to the follower conquered a similar obstacle. Another path to higher self-efficacy is helping the follower through a mastery experience. That is, the shepherd leader
comes alongside the follower for a while and demonstrates how to
do the task.

Sometimes the problem holding your team or company back is
a person with irritating behaviors. Research on groups and teams
clearly shows that certain behaviors are detrimental to team performance. When one or more team members exhibit behaviors like
negativity, tantrums, attacks, whining, or sniping, it can drain the
rest of the group. Shepherd leaders must first confront the behaviors in an attempt to extinguish them. Should this fail, more than
one leader with whom we spoke while writing this book noted that
the behavior could only be extinguished by forcibly removing the
irritating member from the group. Like a pestilence in a flock of
sheep, one wrong person can drag down an otherwise productive
effort. However unsavory, somebody must intervene, and this somebody is the shepherd leader.

Meg Whitman, CEO of eBay, demonstrates that removing irritants counts at the customer level, too. Under Whitman's leadership, eBay survived the dark valley of the dot-com bust, emerging
profitable on the other side. Along the way, some of eBay's veteran
sellers began to complain about eBay's practice of automatically
referring losing bidders to similar auctions. Although the practice
made sense to the eBay leadership, the sellers were finding it irritating. Whitman and company founder Pierre Omidyar flew to the

seller's city, listened to the story, and stopped the practice two days later. Of course, this one intervention is not solely responsible for eBay's success, but it's indicative of a leader who knows that growth happens when irritants are removed. In the wired community of eBay's sellers, word of such irritant removal travels quickly.

New forms of technology might seem like a daunting affliction to some of your followers. Something as basic as switching e-mail programs can cause a surprising amount of crisis among people who were just beginning to feel a sense of mastery over the former program. A few words of encouragement and a demonstration will certainly do more to empower followers than cynically suggesting that the computer's not going to blow up in their face if they turn it on. Encouraging counsel and patient teaching may be two of the most potent salves in the shepherd leader's medicine kit.

The Great Commissioning

Some irritants are easier to remove than others. For the shepherd in the field, ticks and flies are simple to spot because they attack the outside of the sheep. Worms and other internal parasites are much more difficult to diagnose. The same principle holds true for shepherd leaders. Some irritants, like technology glitches, parking difficulties, or problem people, will be obvious. Others will be much more elusive. One hard-to-spot irritant is a negative—or even non-existent—self-image. So another way to look at an anointing is to see it as a way of giving followers a more positive vision of their role in the company. We call this giving of a new personal vision a *commissioning*.

The notion of a commissioning is both ancient and powerful. While still a young man, the Psalmist David was commissioned by the prophet Samuel. Samuel anointed David in his family's presence and proclaimed him the next king of Israel. Although he didn't assume the throne for many years, David moved forward with a greater sense of destiny from that day on.

A more modern example of a commissioning is illustrated in a story from the life of Rabbi Shlomo Zalman Auerbach, the recently deceased rabbinic scholar from Jerusalem. A father and mother came to Rabbi Auerbach seeking his counsel about removing their mentally handicapped son from their home and placing him in a special school. This is a gut-wrenching decision for any parent to make, and these parents were wise to seek counsel from Rabbi Auerbach, as he was known for both his great intellect and his great kindness.

Halfway through the conversation, Rabbi Auerbach grew concerned that the child would feel more betrayed than nurtured by his parents' actions. So he called the boy before him and did something rather unexpected.

"What is your name?" the rabbi asked the boy.

"Akiva," the child replied.

"How do you do, Akiva? My name is Shlomo Zalman Auerbach. I am the greatest Torah authority of this generation, and everyone listens to me." The parents were a bit shocked by this proclamation, as the rabbi was also known for his great humility. He continued, "You are going to enter a special school now, and I would like you to represent me and look after all of the religious matters in your new home. I shall now give you rabbinical ordination. This will make you a rabbi, and I want you to use the honor wisely."

Following his rabbinical ordination, Akiva went to his new home with a fresh sense of identity and mission. He flourished at the school and rarely wanted to leave the campus, even for a weekend, as there might be a question from someone that needed to be answered. Such is the power of a commissioning given from leader to follower.

Self-image is a powerful catalyst for changing behavior due to its strong relationship to behavior. That is, the mental image we have of ourselves has a potent effect on our everyday actions. A person who sees himself or herself as a poor speller will misspell words more often than someone who views himself or herself as a perfectionist (even though both self-images are extreme views). A commissioning is nothing more than helping followers see themselves in a new light with a different self-image. Once he was anointed, the Psalmist David could not help but to see himself as the future king of Israel, and this helped carry him through some difficult times getting there.

Though a seemingly ancient practice, commissionings still occur on a regular basis in modern times. Police officers, firefighters, soldiers, and physicians—to name members of just a few professions—still take an oath when they finish their training. The political world is rife with commissionings, as presidents, justices, and even jury members take oaths when they serve. Graduations and wedding ceremonies could be thought of as commissionings, too. The College of Business Administration at Abilene Christian University goes a step further and conducts a daylong retreat called the Senior Blessing where faculty, parents, and alumni can gather to bless and commission graduating seniors. Such practices send graduates into the world with a greater sense of mission in addition to a diploma.

So what might a commissioning look like in practice for the modern shepherd leader? First of all, a commissioning is more than just a positive performance review. A common management practice is to start performance reviews by stating a number of positive things about your follower's performance this past year. Supposedly, this builds the follower's esteem before the knife is slipped in when the negative aspects of the performance are reviewed. A commissioning is more than just reviewing the follower's job success. In fact, a commissioning should be as non-job-related as possible. Of course, it can happen in the work context, but it should seek to affirm the whole person instead of just approving the person as he or she is valued by the organization.

Whenever possible, shepherd leaders should try to make times of commissioning as ritualistic as budget cycles. Employment anniversaries or traditional holidays might be good times for such an activity. A personal commissioning is always an ideal, but a corporate commissioning can suffice should an individual one prove impracticable. Should the leader just feel too uncomfortable in the role of commissioner, perhaps he or she could call in a minister or clergyman to do it. At a minimum, the commissioning should be done in the presence of the follower. For greatest impact, it should be as public as possible. Job transitions are also excellent times for such commissionings. Imagine the power of going into a new job with the public blessing of your leaders as opposed to hurriedly moving your boxes to a new office and running even faster.

In the end, anointing carries a double meaning for the shepherd leader. At times the shepherd leader anoints in the medical sense to remove irritants. At other times the shepherd leader anoints in the pastoral sense to commission followers. Both are necessary and can greatly improve the quality of life among your followers. More important, neither are things your followers can do for themselves. Followers need shepherd leaders to both commission them and to remove irritants and obstacles they cannot remove themselves.

Shepherd Thinking

- ✒ What might be the three most irritating things about your workplace? Try to come up with a list of three to five items.
- ✒ What might be the most irritating things about you as a leader? Try to come up with a list of three to five items.
- ✒ What negative self-images might your followers have of themselves? (Examples: failure, loser, second-rate performer)
- ✒ What positive self-images might you be able to give them via a commissioning? (Examples: shepherd, gifted)

Shepherd Doing

- ✒ Contact two or three leaders who do work similar to yours. Ask them about a successful removal of an irritation among their followers. See if you can do the same among your followers or if their stories inspire a new way of removing some of the irritations you listed in "What? Reflections."

☛ Consider doing a 360-degree performance feedback to learn how your followers view your strengths and weaknesses as a leader. Look at your perceived weaknesses in light of the irritations you listed, and make changes if necessary.

☛ Find an appropriate forum in which to give a commissioning to some of your followers. Job changes are often a good time to do this, but there may be others. Write down your blessing, and speak it to your follower in either a one-on-one meeting or in a company or work group meeting.

Chapter Ten

Shepherds Create Supply

My cup runneth over.

Here's a little secret about you—your life is dominated by "demands." When you awaken in the morning, you are already behind. If you have time to prepare them, you spend your day working through endless series of lists: to-do lists (for yourself), must-do lists (at work), honey-do lists (around the house), and the like. You probably record the daily demands of life in a schedule book or calendar, which is roped to your body like an anchor. One friend carries a five-year calendar in his pocket! Then after racing through your day, your head hits the pillow at night, not counting sheep but listing all the demands you did not meet.

You see, when life is lived from the demand side, somehow the cup is never quite full. There is always one more duty, one more obligation, one more needy person. The bottomless in-basket of demands is never fully exhausted, though you are. When you run daily life as a rat race, you never quite reach the elusive finish line. To avoid wipe-out, you have to get off the track—for a day off, a vacation, or, worst-case scenario, a hospital stay. You may feel like the man who kept getting home late from work and missing the family dinner. When chastised by his nine-year-old daughter, he explained that Daddy really wanted to be home with the family, but he just had more work than he could finish. Unimpressed, she replied, "Maybe they need to put you in a slower group." How many times have you wished that for yourself?

The Shepherd's Cup

By contrast, the writer of Psalm 23 has found an entirely different approach: supply-side living! When he looks at his life, he says simply: My cup runs over! Another translation of the psalm says, "My cup is filled to the brim." When combined with his earlier statement—"I shall not want"—the picture that emerges is one of a happy and contented sheep. Not only are the demands of life fulfilled, but the supply is one of real abundance. Now we all have days when life is good, but one senses that this sheep has found a way to frame life more consistently from the supply side. Reflections like "I shall not want" and "my cup runneth over" suggest one who has learned that life is not all wearying demands.

If your life were depicted as a cup, what would it look like? Would it be full of holes and leaking? Might it be cracked from the daily grind? Perhaps you find yourself yearning for a larger cup that might hold more. Maybe you feel that if you only had a smaller cup, it would be full. The shepherd's cup reflects a mentality of abundance, in which supply not only meets but happily exceeds the demands of life.

Personomics

Families, corporations, and governments have all learned the painful lesson that in building a budget, supply and demand must eventually balance. But after centuries of working mainly to limit the demand side (expenses), the great economic discovery of recent years is that increasing supply (revenue) is another powerful way to balance a budget. The tax rebate Americans received in the mail is but one way that "supply-side economics," adopted in some form by two-thirds of the nations of the world, seeks to stimulate the economy and increase financial supply.

Similarly, supply and demand must balance in our personal lives. For every activity that drains us, there should be something that supplies us. Whenever we deplete the supply, we must, without great delay, find a way to restore it. Perhaps we should call this approach to life "personomics," acknowledging that there is a kind of supply-and-demand economics that applies to the lives of people, especially leaders.

If you are honest with yourself, you know that just managing the demands of life is never enough. On your bookshelf, alongside the diet books that once held such great promise for limiting your girth, you will probably find a collection of tools that seemed like they would finally help you get a grip on your time. Elaborate calendar systems, organizers, notebooks with task systems—they're all there. And yet the demands keep piling up at an ever-increasing pace.

One reason just managing tasks doesn't bring life into balance is that you are still focused only on the demands themselves. Try this experiment, taught to aspiring trial attorneys in law school. Close your eyes. Now, do *not* think of a blinking red light. Think about anything else, but not a blinking red light. Of course, the only thing you can think of is that silly red light. This exercise, which alerts prospective lawyers that telling a jury to disregard something often causes them to remember it all the more, also illustrates one of the limitations of time and task management tools: they focus the mind ever more on your burdens. One of the things lawyers and accountants hate about their work is keeping time sheets. They are efficient, but they are just one example that the very tools that help you manage time and tasks can also weigh you down.

Another reason demand management alone isn't sufficient is that it is not just the sheer number of tasks or even the time they require that is burdensome. Often it is the rut that demands carve into your life that is so discouraging and even debilitating. Some mornings, just waking up feels like the movie *Groundhog Day*, in which Bill Murray was consigned to living the same day over and over again. You wake up, you're already behind, you want to exercise or meditate but there's not time, the kids are hungry, the car needs gas, you're late to work. Here we go again. All the calendars and organizers in the world won't pull you out of that rut. What

William Willimon, dean of the chapel at Duke University, said about ministry is true of leadership and life more broadly: "Burnout in ministry results not from overwork but from undermeaning." Balancing your life is as much about increasing the supply, filling the cup, as it is about managing the demands. Here's an illustration that might help clarify the concept:

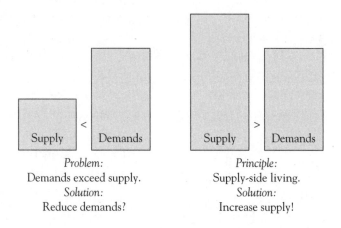

Problem:
Demands exceed supply.
Solution:
Reduce demands?

Principle:
Supply-side living.
Solution:
Increase supply!

It is odd, then, that we somehow feel guilty or lazy when we think about taking time for our cup to be filled. Everything else in life needs to be supplied and renewed. Did you remember to plug in your cell phone when you got home, recharge your razor, renew the battery supply for your computer? For David, it was as a Boy Scout on a first camping trip that the lesson of renewal came home so clearly. Collecting the wood and starting the fire was one thing, but staying up all night in shifts to keep it renewed was something else. Filling the cup is not just a luxury; it is half of the vital supply-and-demand cycle of life.

Increasing Your Supply

All great leaders must, at some point, figure out their sources of supply and when and where to get them. President Bush, for example, finds his supply at his ranch in Texas. When he can't travel that far, he has found that a weekend at Camp David or even a jog on the White House grounds will do. It wouldn't be high on everyone's list of cup fillers, but President Reagan liked to clear brush at his small ranch in California. (Some wags wondered in amusement who had the contract to provide all the brush for him to clear!) Sam Walton was energized by visiting his Wal-Mart stores. Winston Churchill, the great "lion" leader of World War II England, took a daily nap. One leadership couple holds that for them, "All happiness depends on a leisurely breakfast."

What about the rest of us, who don't have ranches and can't take naps in the middle of the day? How do we increase supply and find our cups full to overflowing? First, begin to identify and give thanks for your rich supply. Spend at least some time every day, preferably before the demands hit, by taking inventory and giving thanks for the abundance that is yours. Invest as much time counting and appreciating the revenue side of your personal ledger as you do managing the expense side. Regard your blessings not like the lunch bag of chips that shrinks to a mere handful after the air is removed but more like that Styrofoam packing material that fills a shipping carton. Like much of life, supply-side living is in large measure a mental attitude. To some, the same cup is half empty, to others half full. Having your cup filled to the brim starts by recognizing and appreciating what you have as much as or more than what you owe.

Next, focus on activities in your day that energize you. As a university president, for example, David most loved teaching and dealing with students. When colleagues asked why he would add teaching to the huge stack of demands on his desk, he explained that it was the one thing that gave him the energy to tackle the rest of the pile. You see, the very activity that may be a draining demand for some people can be a source of energizing supply for others. For one friend, all of life works better with a clean garage, so you'll find him there on Saturday mornings. By contrast, a cluttered garage is just fine with another, who instead feels better with her bills paid and checkbook balanced (OK, at least close to what the bank statement says), so that's what she does on Saturday morning. For these people, these tasks are not burdens but sources of supply. Know where to find energy and supply in your daily activities, and be sure to go there. If there's nothing in your job that energizes you, you'd better start looking for a new job!

Do not fail to spend time with the people in your life who supply you. There are people who drain you of energy and people who supply it. To put it another way, some people bring joy *wherever* they go, and some bring joy only *when* they go. Do not spend all of your week with the people who need you and want you, important as they are; also give yourself permission to be with the people who excite and energize you. In peer counseling, David has found that when people are feeling stressed out and at their limit, they are generally spending the overwhelming majority of their week with people who take energy and very little with those who give it. You will be surprised how much more you can share with others when your own cup is filled to the brim by the people who can supply you.

Then, too, return to places that give you energy. Do you know of a place where, at least for you, the air is different, somehow life-giving? Is there a place of solitude where your heart beats more contentedly and your mind thinks in fresh ways? There is a spirit of place, a role for space in our lives, and we need to be able to find these places and spaces and return to them for refreshment. When David and his family returned from a sabbatical in an English village and described the very special feeling he had there, a friend suggested that he could also find a place like that closer to home, and he did, at the beach. For years he made regular, if brief, visits to that beach and occasional return trips to that village. Maybe you should arrange to work outside your office in a special place a day or two a month. You must find and return to those places that give you energy.

It is amazing that we live in a time when people are energized and increasingly effective in their careers, but their personal lives are often characterized by fatigue, dullness, and worry. Much of this is because we do not allow our cups to be filled by supply-side living. Someone has said that today's executives read only in their own fields, play only to relieve stress, eat only to make business contacts, and vacation to re-create in shorts the same stresses they experience the rest of the time in business attire. Increasingly, the important resource in almost every field is human capital, that is to say, highly trained, motivated, effective people. That must include people whose lives are well supplied, whose cups are filled to the brim, ready to go.

The Rhythm of Supply-Side Living

There is, of course, a rhythm to all of this. Just as we breathe out, we also breathe in. The well is emptied, but then it must be refilled. Everyone can't find large doses of supply every day, but think in terms of balancing out your week. Be certain to schedule some of those energy-giving activities, and spend time with supply-side people, at least every week. Then, every month, plan to go to some place that is a source of supply for you. Breathe its life-giving air; allow your cup to be filled to the brim. Once a year, plan a major time away, a real vacation. Don't just visit relatives or clean the garage, unless those happen to be major sources of supply for you; truly unplug from the demand side and recharge your batteries. If you're really fortunate, you might even plan a sabbatical every decade or so, taking several weeks or months to recalibrate mind, body, and spirit from the demands of life.

To be able to care for the sheep, the shepherd must learn to care for himself. It is not fair, but people notice and comment on whether the leader seems tired or edgy. Followers do not like their leader to seem tired or sick. The care and feeding of the shepherd, then, becomes a matter of importance for the entire flock. In setting a tone for the organization, it may well be that the leader doing fewer things with energy and enthusiasm will be of greater value and importance than doing more things with less passion or enthusiasm. In that sense, leaders must accept that they are assets worth caring for and keeping well supplied.

Michael Novak's "Legend of the Bay Steed" teaches this lesson so clearly. A wounded knight returned home on his sturdy bay steed, a horse that was widely admired for its strength and beauty. The knight gave the steed freedom for most of the day, but he occasionally gave permission for it to pull heavy loads no other beast in the village could haul. When the knight died, villagers used the horse regularly and gave him less freedom and care. But very soon, the bay steed grew ill and died, with many unfinished tasks left in the village. The townspeople had neglected the knight's instruction: "It is important for the steed to feed quietly and gambol at will around the meadow in which he is fenced." Without this regular supply, the horse could not meet the villagers' demands.

Supply for Followers

Having found ways of increasing their own supply, shepherd leaders must then be attentive to supply for the flock. This challenge is closely related to the call of Chapter Two, "Shepherds Meet Needs," and is nicely reflected in the images of green pastures and still waters. But there may be times when sheep become so stressed that they will not eat or drink, even when the resources are nearby. They say you can lead a horse—or sheep—to water, but you can't make it drink. Well, sometimes you have to remind the sheep of the importance of replenishing supply. It's like the exercise leader who every once in a while says, "Remember to breathe." It seems obvious, and yet we sometimes become so busy, so preoccupied, so pressed that we forget the cycle of supply.

With her television program, magazine, movie production division, and other lines of business, Oprah Winfrey oversees a large corporate empire, Harpo Inc. She acknowledges that in the early days she worked people too hard but has since learned that building more supply into people's lives creates greater overall productivity. Employees receive an average of six weeks' vacation in their first year, and there is an in-house spa and gym at headquarters. In return, the company has only modest turnover (10 to 15 percent per year), and the average tenure of its senior executives is ten years.

Similarly, Ben Cohen and Jerry Greenfield, better known simply as Ben and Jerry, developed their ice-cream company in a way that built supply for them as well as their people. They believe that work should be rewarding in itself, adopting the unofficial motto "If it's not fun, why do it?" They carefully incorporate their values in all they do, including earmarking 7.5 percent of all pretax profits for charitable donations and involving a team of employees to make the giving decisions. Organizing the company around their own values provided a powerful source of personal supply.

The need for supply-side living in our day is, ironically, captured in an old story. Lettie Cowman, in her book *Springs in the Valley*, tells of Westerners who had come to travel in Africa in an earlier day. Tribesmen had been arranged to carry their considerable baggage as they traveled. The first day went in Western style: too far, too fast. The next morning, the tribesmen just sat, refusing to go forward. After some discussion, the reason was translated to the Western visitors: they had to wait for their souls to catch up with their bodies. At some deep level, the Africans understood the lesson of shepherd leadership, that human beings work efficiently only when supply integrates with demand, when soul integrates with body, when the cup is full, even to overflowing.

Shepherd Thinking

- ☞ Can you list a few friends who give you energy? Do you spend as much time with them as with the people who drain your energy?
- ☞ Do you have certain places where you feel better, more relaxed? How often do you go there?
- ☞ What do you most enjoy in your job or daily tasks?

Shepherd Doing

☛ Check your calendar for the past month. Do you have some appointments every week with people who give you energy? If not, make a change this week.

☛ Have you been to your special place this month? If not, plan to go before the month is out, even if only for a few hours.

☛ Examine your calendar, and make an honest assessment of your supply versus demands. Make changes for the coming weeks.

Chapter Eleven

Shepherds Share a Positive Vision

Surely goodness and mercy shall follow me all
the days of my life.

As David and Sally Davenport discovered, living in a college president's campus residence is a mixed blessing. Although the Brock House on Pepperdine's Malibu, California, campus is a fabulous home, living there involved hosting as many as five thousand guests per year, from students to Supreme Court justices.

David recalls inviting a few campus administrators to a small dinner one evening in honor of Norman Cousins, a brilliant author, editor, and thinker. Midway through the meal, Cousins decided it would be fun to go around the table and ask each guest to summarize what he or she had learned in life in a single statement. You can imagine the discomfort, and even terror, as guests faced such an unexpected and difficult request.

It turns out that Cousins frequently asked world leaders the same question. One of his favorite responses came from Soviet leader Nikita Khrushchev, who said, "Never turn your back." *Tonight Show* host Johnny Carson asked renowned business leader Conrad Hilton to look into the television camera and tell the nation what he had learned in years of running major hotels. Hilton had obviously considered such matters and quickly cut to the heart of things: "The shower curtain goes inside the tub."

Oliver Wendell Holmes would have called these summaries "the simplicity on the other side of complexity." More specifically, he said: "I would not give a fig for the simplicity on this side of complexity, but I would give my life for the simplicity on the other side of complexity." Many people in life settle for the simple, shallow view of things. Some work harder to probe the deeper complexities of life but often bog down and live in perpetual confusion and uncertainty. A few work their way through the complexity to find a handful of organizing principles to help them master it. Our best thinkers and leaders discover Holmes's simplicity on the far side of complexity.

Shepherd Simplicity

At first glance through contemporary eyes, the Psalmist shepherd sounds a bit naïve when he writes, "Surely goodness and mercy shall follow me all the days of my life." These sentiments seem, at the very least, out of touch with the realities of twenty-first-century life. After all, ancient shepherds knew nothing of cancer or Alzheimer's. They lived centuries removed from stock markets crashing on retirees and airplanes crashing into office towers. Surely those are not part of a life of goodness and mercy.

But wait! Before we conclude that expecting a life of goodness and mercy is out of touch with modern realities, consider how we might have coped with the hazards of ancient life. How might we react when we saw our flock and livelihood wiped out by disease? Is having your assets fall off a mountain trail or die in childbirth any easier than watching your investments dwindle in an economic downturn? Would you really be prepared to trade your king-sized mattress for a bedroll on the hard ground or your daily hot shower for an occasional dip in the river or pond?

No, if we are unable to identify with the shepherd's perspective that goodness and mercy will surely be his, it is not because he lived an easy life and did not know hardship. Nor is it because he had a case of the simples and was unfamiliar with complexity. As Psalm 23 reaches its conclusion, the shepherd has surmounted hardships and broken through complexities to develop a positive and useful frame for dealing with life. If we cannot join him in recognizing the constancy of goodness and mercy in life and leadership, developing a positive vision is where we need to work.

Leaders Share a Clear and Positive Vision for Their Followers

One of the crucial choices of leadership—and life—is whether to live in reaction to circumstances or whether you can develop a positive vision into which you will fit the events and circumstances of life. If you were to distill the essentials of leadership into a few simple points, this would be one of them: people want to follow a leader with a clear and positive vision about the future. Line up two shepherd leaders, one whose constant refrain is "The enemy is on our tails, and we need to move forward quickly" and one who says, "Surely goodness and mercy shall follow us, so let's move ahead." They will pick shepherd leader number two every time.

American voters confirmed this strong preference in 1980 when they elected the optimist Ronald Reagan over President Jimmy Carter, whose leadership was perceived as too pessimistic. While Carter spoke in detailed terms about America's problems and limitations, Reagan painted the nation's future with a broader and more hopeful brush. Critics wondered whether Reagan's approach was sometimes too simplistic or Pollyannaish, but the voters had little doubt which leader they preferred to follow. Historians credit Reagan with many accomplishments, but one of the most important is restoring America's sense of confidence and optimism.

There are three elements of this kind of visioning or framing. First, it is aimed toward the future: goodness and mercy *shall* follow me all the days of my life. Shepherds are out in front leading the flock, and the vision of the future they communicate is central to that leadership. The pilot must be in the front of the plane looking forward and communicating about the path ahead, and not staring in rearview mirrors or out the back window. At fast-growing Mostly Muffins, Inc., CEO Molly Bolanos emphasizes "managing forward."

When executives meet to look at critical numbers, they do so with a view to the future, anticipating roadblocks and planning the course ahead. "People get excited by keeping their eyes up and out, instead of down," she says. People need a hopeful vision about the future of the organization and their role in it.

A second element of the vision is that it must be positive. Here leaders walk a bit of a tightrope because they need to be positive but not unrealistic. As America deals with difficult economic news, for example, political cartoonists love to lampoon those whose view of things is so rosy as to be unrealistic. Shepherd leaders know that there will be rough terrain, that green pastures and still waters may be scarce, that disease may strike the flock. Still they find a way to frame a positive yet realistic vision of the future. Where might the shepherd leader fall on the spectrum of pessimist-realist-optimist? We should join Norvel Young, longtime chancellor and president of Pepperdine University, in ruling out the pessimist option. He frequently said, "I don't know enough to be a pessimist."

A very interesting body of research confirms this approach. In *Learned Optimism*, psychologist Martin Seligman argues that he can predict business, political, and personal success by ranking people on an optimism-pessimism scale. For example, new sales staff at MetLife who scored higher on learned optimism sold 37 percent more life insurance in their first two years than those who scored as pessimists. Seligman demonstrates an ability to predict the results of political campaigns based on voters' preference for optimism. Optimists are more resistant to disease. Best of all, he says, optimism can be learned.

Probably the right point on the scale for a shepherd leader is to be a realistic optimist, setting a positive yet plausible vision of the future. People need to know that leaders are aware of the difficulties and challenges and that they are not being ignored or masked. Leading an Internet company when the dot-com bubble burst created many challenges. When David was CEO of Starwire, he learned that some staff members felt that his monthly briefings on the company's condition were too positive, perhaps even misleading. At first, David felt angry at not being trusted but, on reflection, he realized that his own need to view things optimistically was not shared by everyone. At his next briefing, he presented things as an optimist might see them, then as a pessimist would view them, and finally concluding with the middle ground of a realistic optimist. Often the leader's frame is as important as the content.

A third dimension of the positive vision is that it should be simple and clear. Do you recall your driver's training classes, where the instructor was constantly challenging you to "get the big picture"? In a classic case of finding the simplicity on the far side of complexity, the challenge was to take in a lot of data, not only about your position on the road but also about road conditions and the locations and actions of perhaps dozens of other drivers. The details of steering, accelerating, and braking fell into place when you focused on a point well down the road and saw the big picture. When President John F. Kennedy said we would land a man on the moon and bring him home safely within the decade, that provided a simple and clear vision for America's space efforts. When Sam Walton stated that Wal-Mart would double the number of stores and increase the sales volume by 60 percent per square foot by the year 2000, that gave a clear, albeit challenging, vision of where the company was headed.

It is often a good idea to test the confidence of the flock in this vision. Especially when developing a new vision, take aside some of the leaders of the organization and let them respond to the concept. One business leader found that a secret ballot, in which team members rate their confidence in the achievability of the approach on a scale of 1 to 5, can be revealing. More than once, leaders have gotten caught up in their own visions and ideas only to find that the leadership team does not really have confidence in them. As someone said, many a young leader has gone out to set the world on fire only to return for more matches. If your fellow leaders do not have strong belief in the vision, either adjust it or find new managers who do.

How to Frame the Bad with the Good

If framing a positive vision is one of the most important aspects of life and leadership, figuring out how to incorporate bad things within that frame is one of the most difficult. Rabbi Harold Kushner hit a responsive chord with his book *When Bad Things Happen to Good People*. As Kushner pointed out, this is an important problem because bad things not only have an effect on the good people who suffer from them but also on those who want to believe that the world is essentially just and fair. How, then, does the shepherd leader learn to deal with misfortune and evil and still say that life is basically attended by goodness and mercy?

For starters, we must note that the Psalmist doesn't say that everything that happens in life is good but rather that goodness and mercy follow him. Yes, predators from the outside and disease from the inside can occasionally break through, but the basic frame of his life is one of goodness and mercy. David Davenport's father was a baker, and he recalls, as a boy, watching his dad at the mixing bowl. All kinds of unappetizing ingredients would go in—dry flour, raw eggs, overripe bananas. But a wonderful product, banana bread, would emerge. It's not that every ingredient in life is good but that they may all come together to produce a beautiful life. A popular saying today— "It's *all* good"—conveys the same sense, that life has its ups and downs but they work together to produce a positive and productive whole.

Leaders, then, learn to reframe bad things into a part of the more positive whole. Reframing, or simply learning to look at things from a different or larger perspective, is an important tool in the leader's kit. Learning to see things from different perspectives is taught in children's math classes these days. For example, if you were to add 28 plus 41 quickly in your head, some people might simply add the two columns. Others would reframe the problem and add 30 plus 40 and then make an adjustment for the rounding. Still others might add 20 plus 40 and then 8 plus 1. Learning to see problems from multiple perspectives allows the leader to see challenges in new and useful ways.

Reframing into a larger perspective can be even more helpful in dealing with bad news. There are several questions the leader should ask, in fitting difficult developments into a more positive whole. For example:

- How important will this be one week, one month, or one year from now? This is a way of gaining perspective on the long-term impact of the bad news.

- Is there a silver lining in this cloud? Most bad developments have at least an element of good, and it is often possible to tease that out and expand on it.

- In what way will this make me or the organization stronger? Surviving tough times usually strengthens us, and our ability to focus on that prospect lends a helpful perspective.

- How might I learn from this experience? Most leaders are regularly enrolled in the school of hard knocks, and sometimes the value of the learning exceeds the tuition of suffering we may pay.

- Might this draw our team together more closely? Families and teams usually grow together to fight adversity, so hardship needs to be recognized as a relationship opportunity.

- Will there at least be a good story from this down the road? One leader says that at the very least, he can always get a good lesson or an interesting story out of problems he encounters.

Do Good Things Happen to Good People?

If bad things happen to good people, but the people learn to frame them in a positive vision of life, is it also true that good things happen to good people? More specifically, do good things happen to them because they are good people? Do goodness and mercy follow the shepherd because he has learned and practiced the leadership lessons of Psalm 23?

Although there is not a one-to-one correlation between an act of goodness and a comparable reward, the answer would nevertheless appear to be yes, an increased measure of goodness and mercy generally follows the life of a good shepherd leader. Studies have shown that students who are better prepared and feel greater confidence than others outperform the others on tests. Similarly, students with good study habits and discipline over time perform better on standardized achievement tests than those who attempt to prepare at the last minute. In that sense, we have known since we were children that good things happen more often to good people.

It appears that even the dimension of chance or luck follows good people. The word *serendipity* describes the ability to find valuable things unexpectedly. But generally, those who have discovered truly valuable things unexpectedly were at least looking for something, if not for the treasure they found. As Ralph Waldo Emerson once noted, Columbus was looking for a direct route to Asia when he "stubbed his toe on America." Thomas Edison was working on the repeating telegraph when he developed the phonograph. Louis Pasteur, who was searching for a way to keep wine from souring and found pasteurization, correctly concluded: "Chance favors the prepared mind."

Most philosophers agree that even the ultimate goal for most people—happiness—does not come by direct pursuit but by living a good life devoted to something larger. Indeed, perhaps the surest way not to find happiness is to chase it. Only by investing oneself in meaningful activity or service, by developing close and loving relationships, and, for many, believing in a transcendent God does one find happiness. As people in the organization develop good character, good things will surely result. So it does seem to be true that the shepherd leaders, by giving themselves to others and by disciplining themselves as leaders, can expect goodness and mercy to follow, and the flock will also enjoy the fruit of the good character they develop.

Shepherd Leaders Set the Paradigm

The liberating truth for the flock is that the followers' reality is determined not by their circumstances but by their shepherd. Yes, the ground is hard, the grass has been overeaten, and there is no water nearby. True, the enemies of disease and predators are always at hand. But a shepherd defines a new model, a new paradigm for their lives, one of goodness and mercy.

Truly powerful organizational leadership today is not defined by who can give the most orders or issue the largest number of memos. The power belongs to those who set the paradigm, who establish the tone and culture of the organization. Thomas Kuhn, in *Structure of Scientific Revolutions,* used the term *paradigm* to describe the conceptual framework or worldview of particular communities. The fact that Amazon.com lists more than five hundred books with the word *paradigm* in the title attests to its sweeping impact.

As one CEO told us, "Show me the morale of your top thirty people, and I'll show you the morale of your company." By working through the difficulties and complexities of organizational life, shepherd leaders find a framework, a worldview for the flock. By conveying it in positive, clear terms, they begin to set the tone and culture for how people will live and act within the family, the business, the classroom, or wherever leadership is provided.

Shepherds know the valleys and the enemies, but they set a positive tone for dealing with them. It is this vision, this framework, this worldview that attracts commitment and energizes people. It draws the flock together and empowers it to move forward. As John M. Richardson put it, "When it comes to the future, there are three kinds of people: those who let it happen, those who make it happen, and those who wonder what happened." Shepherd leaders are making it happen! Surely goodness and mercy will follow them.

Shepherd Thinking

- If Norman Cousins had asked you to summarize what you have learned in life in one statement, what would you say?
- If Cousins asked you to summarize what your organization is about in one sentence, how would you respond?
- Where would you place yourself on the spectrum of pessimist-realist-optimist? Where would your flock place you?
- Who or what sets the paradigm in your organization?

Shepherd Doing

- Write down your vision as a leader. Ask three coworkers to do the same, and see how closely they match. Is your vision as clear and simple as you think?
- Identify three problems in your organization. How might you help people reframe those or place them in a larger and more positive context?
- Write a one-page description of yourself or your organization for a newsmagazine ten years into the future. Share it with your leadership team or your organization for feedback.

Chapter Twelve

Shepherds Cultivate Loyalty

And I shall dwell in the house of the Lord for ever.

Individual mobility is one of the hallmarks of capitalism. Statistics show that the average American changes jobs every two and a half years. And this movement is not just a result of layoffs, either. Surveys show that 30 percent of Americans are planning to change jobs in the next three years. For younger Americans, this number rises to 60 percent. This desire for mobility among Americans extends beyond the workplace and into the public arena. American citizens can and do threaten to leave the country for a variety of reasons including who will win certain presidential elections. Some may even keep their word and switch countries.

This is a bold contrast to communist nations like the People's Republic of China. In China for much of the past half-century, the Communist Party told college graduates where they were going to work, and you could neither quit that job nor move to another town without the Party's permission—even if your spouse were assigned to a different town. Further still, you could not leave the country without the Party's permission. The former Soviet Union had similar policies concerning individual mobility. No one could move to another city—much less another country—without the permission of the Communist Party. However, the Party members underestimated the desire for mobility among their comrades. When John Ford's film treatment of *The Grapes of Wrath* was released in 1940, the Communist leaders distributed the film throughout the Soviet Union in hopes of showing the dark under-belly of American-style capitalism.

The plan was that their comrades would see the poverty and desperation of the Joad family and be even more loyal to the lead-ers of the Communist Party. Their plan backfired in a rather comi-cal and unexpected way. The Soviet citizens watched the Joad family pile into their automobile for the trek from the Dust Bowl to California and cried out, "Hey, they get to move in America! What a country! And even the poorest people have cars!" In contrast, only the richest and most privileged Soviets had automobiles and could use them to move wherever they desired.

The Soviets' basic mistake was literally treating people like ani-mals. That is, if you force them to stay in one place, they *have* to be loyal to you. This might work with sheep, but it cannot work with freedom-loving humans. Of course, one can signal loyalty by stay-ing in the place for many years—much as one might do in a mar-riage. However, loyalty and mobility are not mutually exclusive. A key concern of the shepherd leader is to cultivate a heart of loyalty among his or her followers.

The Vanquished or the Volunteer?

"And I will dwell in the house of the Lord for ever" is a dangerous way to close out this psalm—or any piece of writing, for that mat-ter. That's because this one line can have two very different in-terpretations. This line might be the final words of a poem of lamentation, one that captures the sentiments of a vanquished soul condemned to a life of servitude in the home of a conquering gen-eral. In such a context, this phrase could be interpreted as the final, despairing words of the author.

Instead, these words capture the gratitude of a person fully aware of the rich life he has enjoyed in the care of a good shepherd. Instead of a cry of hopelessness, it is a public declaration of com-mitment to the good shepherd. This is not the language of the vanquished but the language of one who voluntarily commits to advancing the cause of his leader and wants the world to know.

Such a profession of loyalty tells us something not only about the leader but also about the heart of the follower. It's doubtful that the Psalmist David had anything approaching the level of material comfort we enjoy today. Yet one sees a great deal of gratitude in his shepherd psalm. David's heart is also a humble heart that is quick to point out his dependence on his leader for his entire well-being. Too many of us fancy ourselves individual achievers dependent on no other person for our accomplishments. A pure individualist would have no obligations and would be loyal to no one. Loyalty springs from a grateful heart—a heart that knows it is better off because it has been in the care of a good shepherd.

A Bigger Vision of Loyalty

The stories and statistics that opened this chapter suggest a reality check for every shepherd leader: expect some of your followers to leave your company. Nonetheless, some of us believe that our followers should stick around forever. So just where did our notions of "long service is loyalty" come from? It's a relic of Industrial Age thinking. Prior to the rise of the "Generals"—General Motors, General Electric, General Foods, General Dynamics, and other large corporations—American workers never thought twice about having a "career." Before 1900, few workers experienced the career stability that was the norm for two or three generations in the twentieth century. The advent of the modern corporation reduced both mobility and turnover for the average worker. Instead of constantly moving about the country, we took out a thirty-year mortgage, bought a home, and put down roots. Staying with the same firm for twenty, thirty, even forty years—an unprecedented achievement in economic history—became the norm. Loyalty was prized over all else and demonstrated by not even looking at other job opportunities.

Most of us now snicker at the idea of staying with the same company for forty years; the average American worker now switches employers several times throughout the working years. Ironically, a revolving door for talent is a sign that you're attracting top-notch people to your organization. During a visit to Silicon Valley, an entrepreneur confided in Blaine his frustration concerning the rate at which workers moved in and out of his company. That is, he could scope out talented people for his firm, but these workers would inevitably stay for no more than two years and then move on to another opportunity. In part, it may have been the nature of Silicon Valley; but it may also have been a testament to the leader's ability to attract and hire talented, mobile people.

Blaine challenged him to have a vision of loyalty beyond his payroll. Instead of thinking about himself as the pinnacle, he could learn to view himself as a springboard that launches talented people into the marketplace to create great products and start their own businesses. It's certainly not wrong to hope that your followers stay at your company for as long as possible. Just be sure to temper this hope with the desire to have your departing followers be advocates of the firm once they leave. In this light, the shepherd leader's loyal followers can span numerous companies, industries, and even countries.

Colleges and universities serve as excellent examples for building this kind of boundary-spanning loyalty. Although most people spend no more than four to five years getting a college education, they are often advocates of the school throughout their lives. It's not uncommon to see a picture of a newborn baby dressed in the colors of the family university. As the child continues to grow, their next picture is often in the school football or cheerleading uniform. Some even go so far as to have personalized license plates bearing the logo of their preferred university.

Every college professor knows that he or she has a classroom full of potential alumni, prospective donors, and future parents of the next generation of students at the university—and hence must manage the class with this loyalty in mind. It's the foolish professor that treats even the most immature student poorly, as this same professor will probably meet a pleasant, mature alumnus at a future Homecoming reception—and feel very uncomfortable.

A Special Concern for the Most Dependent

In contrast to the ultramobile professional employees that inhabit many modern companies, there still exists a remnant of people who will never change companies. Some of these people enjoy their work and the steady paycheck that accompanies it. They like their home and their routine, and they simply don't want to complicate their life with so-called developmental moves. These workers might view you as Albert Einstein's wife viewed him. When asked if she understood her husband's theory of relativity, Mrs. Einstein replied that she did not, but she knew her husband and knew he could be trusted.

Although none of our strategic plans have the lofty complexity of Einstein's theories, they may be beyond the care and concern of some of our followers. Surprisingly, these followers know you, know you can be trusted, and will often follow your leadership without question. Although it's easy to focus our attention on the complainers and naysayers, there are going to be people at work who love being there. These people are loyal, content, and often completely silent.

Some of your followers will want to stay with your company not because they are unwilling to change but because they are unable to change. A few might be unable to switch jobs due to certain health insurance requirements. Still others need to stay in a particular location because of their children or an ailing parent. And some of your followers may simply lack the ability to pursue an opportunity at another company. Often these will be among the lowest-paid workers in the organization. Many of us regularly complain about our work and the hassle it brings into our lives, but what if your work was the best part of your week because your life outside of work was so very unrewarding?

A hallmark of shepherd leadership is creating a place of which your least mobile workers can be proud and to which they can be loyal. In a market economy, it's easy to justify the lowest wage possible for these people. In fact, communism predicted that capitalist employers would exploit such workers to the maximum degree, spurring them to revolution. Shepherd leaders defy the prediction of revolution by showing a special concern for the followers with the fewest options.

Aaron Feuerstein defied such prophecies when fire consumed his Malden Mills textile business in Lawrence, Massachusetts, just weeks before Christmas in 1996. Within twenty-four hours of the destruction, Feuerstein assembled his three thousand workers in a local gymnasium and announced that he would rebuild the mill rather than take the insurance money and cash out of the business at age seventy-one. Beyond this, Feuerstein announced to the already shocked workers that their paychecks would continue for at least another month so as not to spoil the holiday season.

Later that would be extended to ninety days, and health care benefits ran an additional ninety days beyond that. His workers not only benefited from the payroll coverage but even more from the decision to rebuild. Without Malden Mills, Lawrence would have become a ghost town, and three thousand workers would have had to go elsewhere to find work. Because of his decision, 90 percent of his workers stayed with the company over the long term, and the town remained vital. Feuerstein, an Orthodox Jew, stated that he did what he did in order to honor God. Such commitment has seen him through both the high times of rebuilding the factory and the low times of financial struggles both before and after the fire.

So how else does one show such special concern? In many ways, it's learning to see life from the perspective of your followers. Maybe their coworkers are the only people who treat them courteously. Maybe the plants and posters decorating the office make it the most beautiful building they visit all week long. Maybe completing their regular job each day is the only sense of accomplishment and closure they feel in a life that's out of control. For some leaders, it may be intentionally creating a special job for a mentally or physically

you is to do the same. First, be the sort of follower that honors your own leaders by praising them for their good shepherding as often as possible. Beyond this, be a shepherd leader whose followers bless you rather than curse you.

Shepherd Thinking

🖝 How do you feel when followers leave your group or company? Do you feel betrayed, or are you glad for their new opportunity?

🖝 What are you doing as a follower to demonstrate your loyalty to your leaders? Do you expect loyalty and not give it yourself?

Shepherd Doing

🖝 Find somebody in your company who is especially dependent on the income from his or her job. Choose to shepherd this person and protect this person from job loss unless it's a last resort.

🖝 Identify two or three people whom you can develop as shepherd leaders.

🖝 Write about the great leaders you've had in your own life. Begin by listing their great characteristics in your own private journal. Later consider writing them a letter of thanks or sharing these characteristics in a more public way.

Epilogue

A Meditation for Leaders

In writing this book, we did something a bit problematic: we broke Psalm 23 into a dozen pieces. We did this to examine Psalm 23 for leadership knowledge, and this is best done piece by piece. Our proverbial left brain loves this type of analytical activity, and we do indeed gain knowledge as a result. Although we can break Psalm 23 into pieces seeking knowledge, the whole of Psalm 23 is greater than the sum of its parts. Something gets lost in the process of breaking the psalm apart. This something goes by a variety of names—insight, intuition, wisdom. Our more intuitive right brain can receive wisdom from Psalm 23 that eludes the grasp of our more analytical left brain. Now that we're at the end of this book, we want to make things whole and challenge you to put Psalm 23 back together.

Psalm 23 is a poem, not a math formula. Poetry has a much softer reputation among business leaders in our number-driven world. Not everyone can be like poet Dana Gioia, current chairman of the National Endowment for the Arts. Before he became a world-class poet, Gioia got his M.B.A. at Stanford and enjoyed a fifteen-year business career culminating in a position as a vice president for General Foods. Like Gioia, great leaders throughout history have been lifted by poetry. Theodore Roosevelt, Thomas Edison, and George Washington Carver were all great lovers of poetry. Presidents Kennedy, Carter, and Clinton each used poetry as a centerpiece of his inauguration. Also, it should come as no surprise that Pope John Paul II, one of the most influential leaders of the past half-century, is also a poet.

Poetry is not a required class in business school, so few businesspeople know how to read a poem for all it's worth. The only poetry most people get is what comes in the mail on greeting cards or the one-dimensional rhyming poetry of children's books. Psalm 23 is great poetry, but it doesn't rhyme, and it is way beyond one-dimensional. Thus we need to understand why poetry matters for leaders. Here's a three-point primer on poetry as a source of truth, imagination, and morality.

Poetry Gives Us Truth Without Statistics

Business leaders need poetry because it gives them a source of truth other than the scientific method. In the science fiction film *Contact*, Dr. Ellie Arroway (played by Jodie Foster) is thrust into an extraordinary encounter with extraterrestrials and returns with no tangible proof that the experience ever really happened. For a while, she suffers a great deal of frustration urgently trying to communicate the importance of her personal experience to fellow scientists and government panels. In the end, she makes peace with her private knowledge and stops trying to convince others of its truth. Dr. Arroway's dilemma is this: she knows more than she can prove. More specifically, she knows that extraterrestrials exist, but she cannot prove it to anyone.

Like Ellie Arroway, we often know more than we can prove. We may know that someone has committed a terrible crime, but we may not be able to prove it in a court of law. We may know that our new business idea is solid, but we often can't assemble enough evidence to prove this to our potential investors. We may know that the human brain is a remarkable organ, but we can't prove just how it's capable of such things as consciousness or imagination.

This is another reason we need poetry. Poetry can teach us a great deal about truth, but it doesn't "prove" anything because the poet knows things that cannot be proved with statistics. Rather, poetry describes a truth that is often difficult, if not impossible, to articulate precisely. That's why Ellie Arroway lamented during her encounter with extraterrestrials that "they should have sent a poet!" instead of a scientist, as she saw things that she couldn't precisely name or explain. Her language faltered, and her science came up short. Poetry bridges this gap not by naming what cannot be named but by pointing to the mystery and suggesting things about it.

As authors, we know more than we can prove. We know that every human has an immortal soul, but we can't prove this to you. We could try to prove it to you scientifically, but we would most likely fail. The scientific evidence for the existence of the soul is quite limited, while the scientific evidence for the existence of a purely material world is quite strong. In fact, if you've slammed your finger in your desk drawer, you've gathered such material evidence.

We also know that leadership matters immensely in our work, even though we may not be able to prove this scientifically the same way we can prove that regular aerobic exercise results in a variety of health benefits. Furthermore, we know that there are better and worse kinds of leadership. This kind of knowing is not the informed opinion of the researcher but the bone-deep conviction of the believer. Science has taught us many great things about leadership as well as human behavior, and we've cited a few such scientific studies in this book. Nevertheless, Albert Einstein noted, "Not everything that counts can be counted, and not everything that can be counted counts." Psalm 23 helps you keep one foot in the spiritual world as you must stand firmly on the other in the material world.

Poetry Challenges Our Imagination

In January 1967, three American astronauts perished in the first great tragedy of the fledgling American space program. The crew of Apollo 1—Gus Grissom, Ed White, and Roger Chaffee—was conducting preflight tests of their spacecraft when a fire swept the space capsule, killing all three crewmembers. In retrospect, the tragedy seemed preventable. An electrical spark had ignited a flash fire in the oxygen-rich environment of the space capsule. Unfortunately, the three astronauts could not escape because the door to the capsule was sealed by a complex series of latches that took ninety seconds to open under ideal conditions and proved impossible to open in an emergency.

An alarmed Congress called for hearings, and Colonel Frank Borman took the stand to testify. Colonel Borman himself was an astronaut and would later go on to command the Apollo 8 mission—the first American space capsule to orbit the moon. When asked by Congress how such a terrible and seemingly preventable accident could have occurred, Borman gave a simple yet insightful answer. He said, "It was a failure of imagination." The space capsule could withstand both the fires of reentry and the cold of outer space, but no one had ever envisioned that a mundane electrical fire before takeoff could take the lives of three astronauts.

Borman's comments suggest that he and the rest of the team at NASA had stopped short of asking, "What if a fire breaks out in the oxygen-saturated capsule before takeoff?" Space travel was an unprecedented endeavor, and the engineers and administrators at NASA had little to guide them in designing the space capsules that would carry their human cargo to the moon and back. Part of the design process was thinking up worst-case scenarios and then redesigning the craft to handle such emergencies. The Apollo 1 tragedy served as an unfortunate but effective source of imagination at NASA, and the Apollo program concluded without further loss of life.

"A failure of imagination." All too often we become comfortable in our daily routines and give little thought to what the morrow might bring. As always, we live in uncertain times. Now more than ever, we need leadership with imagination when thinking about potential threats. We need leadership that can ask tough questions in order to prepare for frightening scenarios. What if a terrorist attacks our headquarters? What if someone put poison in our pain relief capsules? What if we discovered our core product was quietly killing people? What if parents no longer trusted to send their children to our college campus? It may look like worry, but it's really just using the imagination to think of the possible futures and their consequences.

Imagination springs from many sources, tragedy being one. But "What if . . . ?" cuts both ways as an inspirational question. One can ask, "What if the worst happens?" One can also ask, "What if the best happens?" As poetry, Psalm 23 can challenge the imagination of leaders by motivating you to ask "What if . . . ?" more often. Questions like these:

> What if I were a follower as well as a leader?
>
> What if I learned to see life from the perspective of my followers?
>
> What if my followers' needs were unmet?
>
> What if each of my followers had an immortal soul?
>
> What if I could increase my supply?
>
> What if my followers were also my principal spiritual teachers?
>
> What if my followers wrote a poem about me?

Imagination can both contain damage in our world and also create greater abundance. Shepherd leaders do both and need poetry to fuel their imagination.

Sacred Poetry Gives Leaders a Moral Center

Mark Twain once encountered a businessman with a rather notorious ethical reputation. The man bragged to Twain about both his accomplishments and his future goals. He announced that he hoped to one day travel to the Holy Land, climb to the top of Mount Sinai, and read the Ten Commandments aloud. "I have a better idea," replied Twain. "You could stay home in Boston and keep them." Shepherd leadership is not about reciting Psalm 23 for all your followers to hear. Rather, it's about putting your moral center on display each day in the hundred and one interactions you have with people in your organization.

As authors, we believe that humans are more than just clever animals. We believe that humans are a fundamentally different creation—something considerably more wonderful than sheep. At the same time, humans are also capable of a cruelty and depravity that sheep could never achieve. Sacred texts like Psalm 23 not only help keep our depravity in check but can also inspire us to live up to the nobility of our creation. Czech Republic President Vaclav Havel noted that leaders must have the courage to breathe moral and spiritual motivation into everything.

One of the realities about businesspeople is that they can be extremely results-oriented. The "what's measured gets done" mentality has dominated business for over a century, and it shows no sign of slowing down. Poetry, especially sacred poetry, does not give us a checklist of results but rather presents a moral ideal toward which to strive. It reminds us to focus on rightness and not results in a "show me the money," metrics-driven society. Business does a good job of keeping us focused on results. Psalm 23, in contrast, does a good job of keeping us focused on what is right.

At times the role of the shepherd leader will appear to be entirely worthless in the sense that it achieves no immediate or visible result. Ancient shepherds suffered the same dilemma, in that much that mattered most to the shepherd was unobservable and uncontrollable. These shepherds watched their herds, fed and watered them, managed the breeding season, and hoped that doing the right things in the present would result in a healthy flock of sheep in the future. In the same way, shepherd leaders cannot depend entirely on the hope of visible results.

It would also be a misuse of this text to view it as a recipe for greater health, wealth, and happiness. Although we believe that shepherd leadership can confer some tangible benefits to your business, we offer no "300 percent performance improvement or your money back" guarantee with this book. Rather, shepherd leaders learn to look beyond the observable results to the rightness and truth of their activities. As poetry, Psalm 23 offers business leaders a source of inspiration, a source of truth, and a moral anchor to help you keep your balance in a complex, competitive world.

Toward Shepherd Being

Spiritual disciplines have made a big comeback in recent decades. Starting with Richard Foster's *Celebration of Discipline* and continuing through the *Prayer of Jabez,* faith-centered leaders have been reminded to regularly make time for spiritual matters. For some, it's daily. For others, it's weekly. Still others take a sabbatical once a year for a longer, more intensive spiritual experience. Even our exercise is taking on a spiritual tone as yoga becomes a regular practice for Americans. Prayer and reading of sacred and spiritual texts most likely top the list of most practiced spiritual disciplines. Journaling might sneak in for the spiritual masters among us. In addition to these, we recommend the regular practice of meditation. If prayer is a discipline of speaking to God, meditation is the discipline of listening to God.

Our goal in writing this book is to make Psalm 23 a regular meditation for faith-centered leaders worldwide. The habit of deep meditation and reflection on Psalm 23 will plant it deep within your soul, where it will serve as an unconscious guide for your behavior—or maybe even a conscious check on your behavior when you reach an ethical crossroads. Meditation means spending quiet, reflective time with the entire psalm in order to internalize it and personalize it. It might also be helpful to read and memorize Psalm 23 from the rich variety of translations that exist. We've used the traditional King James Version for this book, but there are many versions of Psalm 23 from which to choose. We've collected a number of them in the Appendix that follows this chapter. Read them all, and find the one that speaks to you.

We meditate because we are finite creatures, quick to forget and easily distracted. Making Psalm 23 a regular meditation means reading the psalm over and over again and reflecting on its words, phrases, and images. The meditation we propose is not about the emptying of the mind. Rather, we advocate a filling of the mind with a deep, sustained reflection on Psalm 23. This type of meditation helps us remove ourselves as the center of the world and makes us available to the reality of another perspective. It helps us gain perspective on ourselves and our problems by viewing them from a good place, a sacred place.

Meditation also helps us regain the wholeness often lost in analytical processes. It can also help us become more integrated beings. Meditation takes our intellectual knowledge of Psalm 23 and connects it to the emotional and visceral side of our lives. Through meditation, we take our knowledge of Psalm 23, use it in our lives, and reflect on it. This process of knowledge, action, and reflection can transform followers into leaders and make already strong leaders into shepherd leaders.

This knowledge-action-reflection path is closely akin to the idea in the opening chapter of shepherd leadership as a way of thinking, doing, and being. As you think deeply on this psalm, the image of the shepherd leader will find a home at the very center of your mind. Once you see leadership differently in your mind, your leadership behaviors will begin to change. As you reflect on your new behaviors, spiritual wisdom begins to take root and a transformation begins. Reading Psalm 23 once from the leadership perspective can introduce you to the image of leader as shepherd. Regular meditation on Psalm 23 can deepen a leader's commitment to the act of shepherd leadership.

Appendix:
Twelve Versions of Psalm 23

Meditations are personal, and a text must be personalized if it is to become a regular meditation for a faith-centered leader. We used the very traditional King James Version of Psalm 23 to frame our chapters in this book because it is the most widely known version. However, this translation of Psalm 23 may not speak to you at your most personal level. Consequently, we've collected a variety of translations of Psalm 23 for you in this Appendix. Some are very contemporary, and others speak of another time, another place, or another people. One possibility is to read through them all until you find the one that speaks most directly to you. Another possibility is to rotate your meditation among the versions seeking new insight in each.

רר

¹ Adonai is my shepherd, I lack nothing.
² He has me lie down in grassy pastures,
  he leads me by quiet water,
³ he restores my inner person.
  He guides me in right paths
  For the sake of his own name.
⁴ Even if I pass through death-dark ravines,
  I will fear no disaster; for you are with me;
  Your rod and staff reassure me.
⁵ You prepare a table for me,
  even as my enemies watch;
  you anoint my head with oil
  from an overflowing cup.
⁶ Goodness and grace will pursue me every day of my life;
  and I will live in the house of Adonai
  for years and years to come.

—*Complete Jewish Bible*

❦ ❦

¹ The Lord is my shepherd, I shall not be in want.
² He makes me lie down in green pastures,
  he leads me beside quiet waters,
³ he restores my soul.
  He guides me in paths of righteousness
  for his name's sake.
⁴ Even though I walk
  through the valley of the shadow of death,
  I will fear no evil,
  for you are with me;
  your rod and your staff,
  they comfort me.
⁵ You prepare a table before me
  in the presence of my enemies.
  You anoint my head with oil;
  my cup overflows.
⁶ Surely goodness and love will follow me
  all the days of my life,
  and I will dwell in the house of the Lord
  forever.

                              —*New International Version*

ɾ ɾ

God, my shepherd!
   I don't need a thing.
You have bedded me down in lush meadows,
   you find me quiet pools to drink from.
True to your word,
   you let me catch my breath
   and send me in the right direction.
Even when the way goes through
   Death Valley,
I'm not afraid
   when you walk at my side.
Your trusty shepherd's crook
   makes me feel secure.
You serve me a six-course dinner
   right in front of my enemies.
You revive my drooping head;
   my cup brims with blessing.
Your beauty and love chase after me
   every day of my life.
I'm back home in the house of God
   for the rest of my life.
                              —*The Message*

❧ ❧

¹ The LORD is my shepherd, I shall not want;
² he makes me lie down in green pastures.
  He leads me beside still waters;
³ he restores my soul.
  He leads me in paths of righteousness
  for his name's sake.
⁴ Even though I walk through the valley of the shadow of death,
  I fear no evil;
  for thou art with me;
  thy rod and thy staff,
  they comfort me.
⁵ Thou preparest a table before me
  in the presence of my enemies;
  thou anointest my head with oil,
  my cup overflows.
⁶ Surely goodness and mercy shall follow me
  all the days of my life;
  and I shall dwell in the house of the LORD
  for ever.

—Revised Standard Version

꠷ ꠷

¹ The Lord takes care of me as his sheep; I will not be without any good thing.

² He makes a resting-place for me in the green fields: he is my guide by the quiet waters.

³ He gives new life to my soul: he is my guide in the ways of righteousness because of his name.

⁴ Yes, though I go through the valley of deep shade, I will have no fear of evil; for you are with me, your rod and your support are my comfort.

⁵ You make ready a table for me in front of my haters: you put oil on my head; my cup is overflowing.

⁶ Truly, blessing and mercy will be with me all the days of my life; and I will have a place in the house of the Lord all my days.

—The Bible in Basic English

❧ ❧

¹ The Lord is my Shepherd [to feed, guide, and shield me],
I shall not lack.
² He makes me lie down in [fresh, tender] green pastures;
He leads me beside the still *and* restful waters. [Rev.7:17.]
³ He refreshes *and* restores my life (my self); He leads me in the
paths of righteousness [uprightness and right standing with
Him – not for my earning it, but] for His name's sake.
⁴ Yes, though I walk through the [deep, sunless] valley of the
shadow of death, I will fear *or* dread no evil, for You are with me;
Your rod [to protect] and Your staff [to guide], they comfort me.
⁵ You prepare a table before me in the presence of my enemies.
You anoint my head with oil; my [brimming] cup runs over.
⁶ Surely *or* only goodness, mercy, *and* unfailing love shall follow
me all the days of my life, and through the length of my days the
house of the Lord [and His presence] shall be my dwelling place.

—*The Amplified Bible*

ꙮ ꙮ

[1] The Lord is my shepherd; I have everything I need.

[2] He lets me rest in green meadows; he leads me beside peaceful streams.

[3] He renews my strength. He guides me along right paths, bringing honor to his name.

[4] Even when I walk through the dark valley of death, I will not be afraid, for you are close beside me. Your rod and your staff protect and comfort me.

[5] You prepare a feast for me in the presence of my enemies. You welcome me as a guest, anointing my head with oil. My cup overflows with blessings.

[6] Surely your goodness and unfailing love will pursue me all the days of my life, and I will live in the house of the Lord forever.

—*The Book*

[1] The Lord is my shepherd.
  I will always have everything I need.
[2] He lets me lie down in green pastures.
  He leads me by calm pools of water.
[3] He gives new strength to my soul for the good of his name.
  He leads me on paths of goodness, to show he is truly good.
[4] Even if I walk through a valley as dark as the grave, I will not
  be afraid of any danger. Why? Because you are with me, Lord.
  Your rod and staff comfort me.
[5] Lord, you prepared my table in front of my enemies.
  You poured oil on my head.
  My cup is full and spilling over.
[6] Goodness and mercy will be with me the rest of my life.
  And I will sit in the Lord's temple for a long, long time.

—English Version for the Deaf

יר יר

¹ You, Lord, are my shepherd.
   I will never be in need.
² You let me rest in fields of green grass.
   You lead me to streams of peaceful water,
³ and you refresh my life.
   You are true to your name, and you lead me along the right paths.
⁴ I may walk through valleys as dark as death,
   But I won't be afraid.
   You are with me,
   And your shepherd's rod
   Makes me feel safe.
⁵ You treat me to a feast, while my enemies watch.
   You honor me as your guest and you fill my cup
   Until it overflows.
⁶ Your kindness and love
   Will always be with me
   Each day of my life,
   And I will live forever
   In your house, Lord.

—Contemporary English Version

¹ The Lord is my shepherd;
  I have everything I need.
² He lets me rest in green pastures.
  He leads me to calm water.
³ He gives me new strength.
  He leads me on paths that are right for the good of his name.
⁴ Even if I walk through a very dark valley,
  I will not be afraid,
  because you are with me.
  Your rod and your walking stick comfort me.
⁵ You prepare a meal for me
  in front of my enemies.
  You pour oil on my head,
  You fill my cup to overflowing.
⁶ Surely your goodness and love will be with me all my life, and I
  will live in the house of the Lord forever.

—The Inspirational Bible, New Century Version

☙ ☙

I

¹ The LORD is my shepherd;
  there is nothing I lack.
² In green pastures you let me graze;
  to safe waters you lead me;
³   you restore my strength.
You guide me along the right path
  for the sake of your name.
⁴ Even when I walk through a dark valley,
  I fear no harm for you are at my side;
  your rod and staff give me courage.

II

⁵ You set a table before me
  as my enemies watch;
 You anoint my head with oil;
  my cup overflows.
⁶ Only goodness and love will pursue me
  all the days of my life,
I will dwell in the house of the LORD
  for years to come.

—*The New American Bible*

𝕣 𝕣

The LORD is my shepherd, I shall not want.
He maketh me to lie down in green pastures;
He leadeth me beside the still waters;
He restoreth my soul.
He leadeth me in the paths of righteousness for his name's sake.
Yea, though I walk through the valley of the shadow of death,
I will fear no evil, for thou art with me;
Thy rod and thy staff they comfort me.
Thou preparest a table before me in the presence of mine enemies.
Thou anointest my head with oil;
My cup runneth over.
Surely goodness and mercy shall follow me all the days of my life,
And I will dwell in the house of the LORD for ever.

—*King James Version*

References

Anderson, L. *They Smell like Sheep*. West Monroe, LA: Howard Publishing, 1997.

Bandura, A. *Self Efficacy: The Exercise of Control*. New York, NY: W.H. Freeman, 1997.

Beckett, J. *Loving Monday*. Downers Grove, IL: InterVarsity Press, 1998.

Cowman, L. *Springs in the Valley*. Grand Rapids, MI: Zondervan, 1997.

Greenleaf, R. *Servant Leadership*. New York, NY: Paulist Press, 1977.

Heifetz, R. *Leadership Without Easy Answers*. Cambridge, MA: Belknap Press, 1994.

Kelley, R. "In Praise of Followers." *Harvard Business Review*, November 1988.

Kuhn, T. *The Structure of Scientific Revolution*. Chicago, IL: University of Chicago Press, 1970.

Kushner, H. *When Bad Things Happen to Good People*. New York, NY: Schocken Books, 1981.

Lewis, C.S. *The Weight of Glory and Other Addresses*. New York, NY: Macmillan, 1980.

Maslow, A. *Motivation and Personality*. New York, NY: HarperCollins, 1954.

Novak, M. *The Fire of Invention*. Lanham, MD: Rowman & Littlefield, 1997.

Palmer, P. *The Courage to Teach*. San Francisco, CA: Jossey-Bass, 1998.

Parker, R. *The Sheep Book*. Athens, OH: Ohio University Press, 2001.

Seligman, M. *Learned Optimism*. New York, NY: Knopf, 1991.

Stone, D. Patton, B., and Heen, S. *Difficult Conversations*. New York, NY: Penguin Putnam, 1999.

White, T. *The Making of the President, 1964*. New York, NY: Atheneum Publishers, 1965.

Acknowledgments

The authors would like to express their appreciation to Mark Kerr and the editorial team at Jossey-Bass, everyone at Yates & Yates LLP in Irvine, California, and the reviewers and managers who helped us shape this book. A special thank-you goes to Keith and Jerry Lynch of Crawford, Texas, for sharing their decades of practical experience in shepherding.

The Authors

Blaine McCormick is an award-winning professor at the Hankamer School of Business at Baylor University where he teaches negotiation and conflict resolution at the undergraduate, graduate, and executive levels. He's the author of two previous books, *Ben Franklin's Twelve Rules of Management* (Entrepreneur Press, 2000) and *At Work with Thomas Edison: Ten Lessons from America's Greatest Innovator* (Entrepreneur Press, 2001), and has published research in a wide variety of academic journals and trade magazines. He is interviewed frequently about his writings, appearing most recently on *CNN* and *ABC World News Tonight with Peter Jennings* and in Harvard Business School's *Management Update* newsletter.

Dr. McCormick began his professional career in Dallas and Plano for ARCO Oil & Gas Company as a human resource management professional. Before joining the Baylor faculty, he held a faculty appointment at Pepperdine University in Malibu, California, where he met his coauthor, David Davenport. He lives in Woodway, Texas, with his wife, Sarah, and three children—Ellis, Miriam, and Bea.

David Davenport has served as president, founder, director, trustee, or chair of more than twenty-five organizations spanning business, education, public policy, law, and ministry, and is currently distinguished professor of public policy and law at Pepperdine University in Malibu, California.

He is a syndicated newspaper columnist, and his articles have appeared in scores of papers, including the *San Francisco Chronicle*,

Los Angeles Times, USA Today, and *Christian Science Monitor.* David has spoken to major audiences worldwide, and has been featured in radio and television appearances.

David Davenport began his career as an attorney and served as President of Pepperdine University during a period of dynamic growth and as CEO of an Internet startup company, Starwire. He and his wife, Sally, have three children.

This page constitutes a continuation of the copyright page.